"*Where is God in All of This?* is just what suffering people need: thirteen simple yet profound biblical reasons why God brings suffering our way for our profit and His glory. Deborah Howard lifts us above our self-centered murmuring to focus on God and our real spiritual profit. Read this remarkable book yourself as a preventative measure before a fresh round of suffering crosses your path, and give a copy to every suffering person you know."
— Joel R. Beeke, president, Puritan Reformed Theological Seminary

"I can't tell you how many times in pastoral ministry I've heard from people—usually out of the crucible of their own acute struggles—who have painfully asked me, 'Where is God in all of this?' Deborah Howard, a trained hospice nurse and a biblical counselor, has done the body of Christ a wealth of good by writing a book that skillfully seeks to answer that very searching question. Combined with a solid biblical understanding of pain and suffering, a mature mind with many years of fruitful ministry to God's hurting people, and a sincere desire to provide critical help to those in need, Deborah has given us a resource of lasting spiritual value."
— Lance Quinn, pastor-teacher, The Bible Church of Little Rock

"Packed with real-life examples coupled with a thoroughly Biblical approach, Deborah's book shows us how we are to properly respond to suffering, and presents to us some of the wonderful things God is doing in us and for us when suffering comes our way. The questions at the end of each chapter help us to think about what she has written and direct us to a godly response when we suffer. Easy to read and packed with tremendous biblical insight, this is a book you will use in your personal counseling and the book you will want to give to hurting people."
— Curtis C. Thomas,
former executive pastor, the Bible Church of Little Rock

"I am grateful to God for the author's faithfulness and obedience to think deeply on this subject and to share the fruit of her meditation with the rest of us. The book is warm, wise, kind, honest, and full of the Word, helpfully applied! Thanks to Deborah for writing it."
— Bob Lepine, vice president, Family Life Today

"This book is no run-of-the-mill theodicy. Rather, it is a beautifully biblically balanced response to the hard questions and challenges that often arise in the contexts of suffering and dying. Howard engages these questions (which often are cast as bold objections) about the sovereignty and character of God both as a seasoned Bible student and as experienced hospice nurse. Her responses are commendable in that while being understanding and compassionate, she never compromises biblical theology. This book is a must for those who are suffering, their family and friends, caregivers, and all of us who will undoubtedly face trials sometime in our lives."

—George J. Zemek,
pastor to seniors and shut-ins, the Bible Church of Little Rock

"Christians who are undergoing suffering need to read *Where Is God in All of This?* They will soon see that the author has been where they are. The title itself resembles the cry of a child of God walking in darkness. In such times everything seems so meaningless—but here, you will find meaning in your suffering and will thank God more than ever before that you are His child. The book's usefulness in pastoral work cannot be exaggerated!"

—Conrad Mbewe, pastor, Kabwata Baptist Church

"It is not Deborah Howard's expertise as a hospice nurse or even her acquaintance with personal pain that makes this book so helpful. Its strength comes from focusing on the Scriptures that encourage us to fully trust God in the midst of heartache and to cling to the perspective that all our trials are indeed 'momentary, light affliction.' "

—Todd Murray, worship pastor, the Bible Church of Little Rock

Where Is God in All of This?

Where Is God in All of This?

FINDING GOD'S PURPOSE IN OUR SUFFERING

Deborah Howard

P&R PUBLISHING
P.O.BOX 817 • PHILLIPSBURG • NEW JERSEY 08865-0817

Page design and typesetting by Lakeside Design Plus

Printed in the United States of America

Library of Congress Cataloging-in-Publication Data

Howard, Deborah, 1952-
    Where is God in all of this? : finding God's purpose in our suffering / Deborah Howard.
        p. cm.
    Includes bibliographical references.
    ISBN 978-1-59638-124-7 (pbk.)
    1. Suffering—Religious aspects—Christianity. 2. Consolation.
3. Theodicy. 4. Suffering—Biblical teaching. 5. Consolation—Biblical teaching. 6. Theodicy—Biblical teaching. I. Title.
BV4909.H68 2009
231'.8—dc22
                                                        2008049655

To the incredible Bible teachers
God has given me,
to my wonderful church,
The Bible Church of Little Rock,
and my precious church family there.

CONTENTS

FOREWORD

Where is God in all this? What do you think God is up to? What do you think He wants to do in your life through these circumstances? These are some of the questions I ask people when they come to me for counseling as they are confronted by unpleasant and undesired circumstances in their lives. My purpose for asking questions like these is to get them to think about God's involvement in what they are experiencing.

In many cases when I've asked these questions I've received a blank stare as if to say, "What are you talking about?" Others have replied with, "I guess I just never thought about that!" In other words, though these people may have been professing Christians, they were living life as practical atheists, or at least as deists who don't think of God as being involved in the running of the world or their lives. Some respond, "I don't have a clue. That's what I've been wondering!" With others, the answer to my question is, "Maybe God is punishing me for something I've done or haven't done. I guess He's angry with me." And then there are those, though they might not want to admit it, who are *upset* with God.

Their theology tells them that God must have had something to do with what is happening, but they conclude that since God is sovereign and He allows these things to happen, it must mean that He really doesn't love or care for them. These people read or interpret God through their own circumstances rather than reading their circumstances through the character of God or through the Holy Scriptures.

When we don't understand what God is up to, we need some solid biblical teaching that will unravel this conundrum for us. I've read and recommended a number of excellent books for people who are experiencing confusion and perplexity as they encounter hard and unpleasant things in life. I, however, can say without reservation that this is one of the best books (perhaps the best) that I have read on the subject.

In this book Deborah, who has known personal suffering in her own life and in the ministry to suffering people in which she has been involved as a hospice nurse for years, shares the results of serious and comprehensive biblical research coupled with real illustrations, examples, and application of the truth. The book is permeated with biblical and practical realism that is extremely insightful and applicable. *Where Is God in All of This?* is an excellent resource for personal study, group study, and counseling assignments for people who need help in understanding where God fits into all that is happening to them and what He may be trying to do in them, through the circumstances they encounter.

I am personally grateful that Deborah's book will be made available, and I intend to use it in all of the ways I have just mentioned. I encourage you to buy it for yourself and others. Read it and apply its truths to your own personal life and in your counseling or teaching ministry. I am sure that, if you devote yourself to reading and using the contents of this book, you and others through you will be personally blessed.

Wayne A. Mack

PREFACE

In February 2005, my first book, *Sunsets: Reflections for Life's Final Journey*, was published by Crossway Books. It has met with moderate success in the marketplace, and I've been gratified to hear, from many of its readers, that it had a positive impact on their lives. That was my prayer from the beginning.

The one chapter people have mentioned time and again is chapter 6, "The Purposes of Suffering." Several pastors are using this chapter in their own counseling work. Churches have used it as a church-wide or class-wide study. And several times I've had requests to make it into a stand-alone book. As a full-length book, *Sunsets* can sometimes be daunting in the face of immediate crisis and is actually designed more to prepare for suffering than to be used as a salve during suffering. Although it can be used for both, I have nonetheless noted the need for a book that speaks only to the purposes of suffering.

Some may think this book is not loving enough, that it doesn't give enough warm fuzzies. Believe me when I say that I am familiar with pain. But I have also come to believe that all the warm fuzzies, all the hugs, and all the "bless your hearts" in the world aren't going to move us beyond our pain. They might make us feel better temporarily, but they're like putting a Band-Aid on a wound. They cover the wound and make it feel better, but they don't *heal* the wound.

God's truth heals the wound. A proper understanding of God and His Word determines our thoughts, our attitudes, and our behaviors. That's why it is important to reflect on the kind of godly issues we'll discuss in the following chapters.

In February of 2006, my darling brother, John Koon, died of lung cancer at the age of fifty-one. I am convinced that the experience of losing him has added greater depth in the rewriting of this chapter and has, therefore, made it better than the original. People grow through adversity. Through suffering they are made progressively more spiritually mature. I think I grew through this experience of loss and pray that God will use it to benefit those who read this book.

Soli Deo Gloria.

ACKNOWLEDGMENTS

I've been blessed by the brilliant, biblical minds God has placed within the circle of my brothers and sisters in Christ. Furthermore, He has blessed me with several who agreed to read this book and provide valuable feedback, suggestions, endorsements, and encouragement: Bob Lepine, Dr. Wayne and Carol Mack, Conrad Mbewe, Todd Murray, Lance Quinn, Curtis and Betty Thomas, and Dr. George Zemek. Thank you.

It has been a tremendous honor, privilege, pleasure, and blessing to study biblical counseling under the direct teaching of Dr. Wayne Mack, whose compassion and godliness oozes from every pore. Thank you for writing the foreword for this book.

My thanks to my dear friends Debbi Casey and Harold and Sue Goss, for being my readers and encouragers for this project, and to Judy Howe for her editorial work.

A special thanks goes to Crossway Books for giving permission to publish a modified version of "The Purposes of Suffering" from my book, *Sunsets: Reflections for Life's Final Journey*, under a new title and with P&R Publishing.

Thank you to Marvin Padgett, who has been instrumental in the publishing of three of my books so far. I couldn't have done it without you.

ACKNOWLEDGMENTS

As always, I'd like to thank my friends and family for their continued support, encouragement, ideas, and suggestions. Your love and friendship is invaluable to me. I'd especially like to take this opportunity to thank my sweetheart for a lifetime, Theron Howard—my husband, my partner in grace, and my best encourager.

INTRODUCTION

We don't have to search very long to find suffering all around us. Each of us has our own problems, heartaches, concerns, and crises. We also witness the suffering of our friends and relatives. By extension, we hear stories about their friends and relatives. We're told of prayer requests for those in our church who are going through trials and sufferings. We hear the concerns of our neighbors and friends. We read the paper or watch the news and hear of one tragedy after another in our city, our state, our country, and the entire world.

This is a certainty—*people are suffering*! The evidence is all around us. But what do we make of it? Why is there so much hardship, illness, pain, and heartache in this world? If God is so good, how can He allow this to happen? What is the answer? What are we to do? Where do the solutions lie to our many problems and troubles? Where is God in all of this?

This book takes a look at how God answers these and other important questions regarding the purposes of suffering. These answers come not from my own weak and finite mind, but from the Bible, the very Word of God.

The book is designed with three parts. Part one covers the theology of suffering, but not as an inaccessible dissertation. Instead, I hope to offer an engaging discussion that will speak to those who struggle to comprehend God's design and plan amidst their pain.

Next, part two reveals the purposes common to all suffering. Every time we undergo a period of trial or adversity, we can be sure that the motives addressed in this section are behind it.

Finally, part three departs from the general and gets specific. Not all suffering is designed for the results described in this section, but I am convinced that God uses our suffering for these reasons *some* of the time. These are very specific purposes, and as such, there isn't as much information given in the Scriptures about them. This fact tends to keep these chapters on the short side, but in no way detracts from their importance.

It is my prayer that this book will help readers to better see their suffering from the perspective of God's principles and designs for our lives and thus to find the path to sweet submission.

General Theology of Suffering

THE PURPOSES OF SUFFERING

Through him we have also obtained access by faith into this grace in which we stand, and we rejoice in hope of the glory of God. More than that, *we rejoice in our sufferings, knowing that suffering produces endurance, and endurance produces character, and character produces hope*, and hope does not put us to shame, because God's love has been poured into our hearts through the Holy Spirit who has been given to us.

—Romans 5:2–5 (emphasis added)

Can We Understand Our Sufferings?

Suffering is everywhere. We ask why, with our eyes turned heavenward and our arms outstretched. "God, can You hear me? Are You paying attention to my prayers? Don't You care that my heart is breaking? If You're such a loving God, how could You let this happen? Where are You in all of this?" Even King David found himself asking,

How long, O LORD? Will you forget me forever?
How long will you hide your face from me?

How long must I take counsel in my soul
    and have sorrow in my heart all the day? (Ps. 13:1–2)

If you find yourself asking these questions, you've probably arrived at a place of heartache and confusion. You know how desperately painful suffering can be—either for yourself or for someone you care about. You're seeking answers and solutions and so far have found none. I hope that is about to change. This little book does not hold miracles that will magically change your situation or heal your broken heart. What it holds is information that leads to hope and peace. And this valuable information comes from the Word of God.

Sometimes when I talk to suffering people about God's Word, they tell me that when a person feels the kind of pain they do, reading a book or hearing a sermon is not going to make them better. Instead of seeking the only true source of comfort that can make a genuine difference in their lives—the Bible—they would rather seek the comfort of the perfect pill or combination of pills. Pills are so much simpler; they take much less effort and if one doesn't help you, there are a multitude of other options. Others turn to the comfort that food or alcohol may provide, but all the pills, food, and alcohol in the world can't give us true peace and comfort. Only God's Word can do that. It is through exposure to His truth that you can find peace in the midst of trouble, hope in the midst of trial, and trust in the midst of chaos. If God gives us the grace to knit our will to His, we can find contentment even in the face of adversity.

Is it an easy thing to conform our will to His? No. In fact, it can only be accomplished through His grace. No matter how many times we try to "be good" our efforts will fail unless we do it through the power of the Holy Spirit. It pleases God when we acknowledge our own weakness, especially in light of His awesome power. In fact, we ought to give thanks for having a God who humiliates our every effort at self-reformation. He is our only genuine Power Source. And it is through prayer and supplication that the Holy Spirit will infuse us with the power to effect lasting changes in our behaviors, attitudes, and lives.

This requires doing something that runs contrary to our human natures. When we experience sorrow and heartache, our tendency is to try to find some way to escape the situation and therefore alleviate the pain. But the answer is not in finding a way of escape or to change everything in our lives that causes us grief. The quest is to figure out how to find contentment *in spite of* our circumstances! We need to acknowledge the utter futility of trying to control all our circumstances, which only brings frustration. Instead, the answer is in changing our *attitude* toward our suffering.

We need to recognize that our circumstances have a purpose! These things don't happen apart from God's sovereignty. So why is He ordering our lives in this way? What are we supposed to learn from this experience? What reason could He have for what He's put on our plates? How can these things possibly work toward our best good, as Romans 8:28 says? We must learn from the trials He gives us. We'll be stronger when we weather the storm and come out on the other side—and by His grace we *can* come out on the other side.

Will we always understand what God is doing through our sufferings? No. However, there are times that He does give us answers when we thoughtfully seek them. It may be immediate or it may take years before we finally realize what He has been doing, though we may never know for sure. Sometimes we find the answers that have previously eluded us through biblical counseling with someone who can responsibly lead us through the Scriptures. But many times we will never know why He sends us through fiery trials—not this side of heaven anyway. Regardless of our understanding, or lack thereof, of the reasons for our suffering, we are commanded to trust Him who holds all things in the palm of His almighty hand. As Proverbs 3:5 reminds us, "Trust in the LORD with all your heart, and do not lean on your own understanding."

Taking a Page from My Own Book

As a hospice nurse I've spent hundreds of hours with suffering people—both the patients and their families. I've heard them express their own version of the questions, "Why is this happening? What did I do to deserve this?" I've witnessed their grief and comforted their sorrowing hearts. I've cried with them and shared the Word of God with them whenever appropriate. One thing I've realized is that when we go through this kind of pain and grief, it is our tendency to feel that we're the only ones going through it, the only ones who hurt like this. Though we always have a tendency to believe the world revolves around us and our little lives, that basic propensity magnifies itself during suffering.

Because I'd had the experience of witnessing grief and death so many times as a hospice nurse, I hoped I would have a somewhat "healthier" reaction. I didn't think that I was superior but that I had gained a handle on these matters. Then my forty-seven-year-old brother was diagnosed with cancer. I wanted to go through this experience with him in an exemplary fashion, not only to help him by being a good sister but in order to glorify God by my attitude and behavior. Of course, there were times when I had to bury my head in my hands and cry, but overall God gave me grace to function when and how I needed to. In the days preceding John's death, my heart felt as though it was being ripped from my body. As I went through the motions of my life, I thought my pain must be utterly transparent to everyone who crossed my path and I wanted to tell every one of them, even complete strangers, "My brother is dying and my heart is breaking."

Sometimes our minister of music at church chooses songs with themes related to our worship service. During those weeks before John died, I felt as though he had chosen the hymns just for me. They were songs of trust and faith that urged me to keep my eyes on my Lord, to bow the knee to His sovereign will, and to place myself into His loving hands. Many times I was unable to sing the words to those much beloved songs and hymns because emotion would grip my heart and tears would stream down my face. All I could do was stand there with my grief exposed, wordlessly praising God and worshiping Him through the lyrics. My heart, ravaged by pain, still clung to Him and trusted Him and poured out to Him the emotion I kept safely hidden most of the time.

Did I feel that I was the only one going through such pain? In a sense, I suppose I did. I remembered all those who I'd walked beside on their own journeys, but somehow, and at some level, I confess I felt it was harder for me. During that time of intense pain, my world revolved around me and my brother. And I'm a professional! A hospice nurse! I was supposed to be spiritually mature and possess an understanding of the purposes of suffering! In fact, I'd already written *Sunsets: Reflections for Life's Final Journey*, from which this book is taken! I guess I thought if anyone could breeze through that experience, I could. I was wrong. I underestimated the intensity of that kind of pain. Losing my brother hurt much more than I'd thought it would.

D. A. Carson eloquently explained this experience in his book, *How Long, O Lord?*:

> But thinking through the theology of suffering, and resolving in advance how you will respond, however praiseworthy the exercise, cannot prepare you for the shock of suffering itself. It is like jumping into a bitterly cold lake: you can brace yourself for the experience all day, but when you actually jump in the shock to your system will snatch your breath away.[1]

No matter how well I thought I had prepared for John's death, I was unprepared when it happened. I had set up some rather optimistic and unrealistic expectations for myself, and in a way I was disappointed. But in another sense, this experience was an incredible encouragement and learning experience to me. In the midst of this heartbreak, I realized that the truths I'd set forth in *Sunsets* held up during the bleakest moments.

Everything I had written gave me confidence, and rereading it ministered to my own wounded heart. I remembered the passages of scripture that related the promises of God, and I was refreshed by them.

It may have been impossible for me to breeze through my experience with an absence of pain, but it was entirely possible to slog through it with my faith and trust intact, understanding that this was not some kind of punishment from God. After all, the Bible never teaches us to be emotionless in the face of suffering. It teaches us to remain faithful, trusting in our Lord to know what's best and to do whatever His perfect will demands. That held true for me while on this journey of discovery. In fact, I rested in the knowledge that everything happened according to His will for my brother's life, for his family's life, and for my own. The grace of God upheld me even through the hardest times. While I experienced incredible pain in saying goodbye to my brother, by the grace of God, my sense of peace and contentment never faltered.

I'm not someone writing a book from a lofty plane above my readers. I'm standing right there among you proclaiming that the truths contained in this book helped me through *my* fiery trial, and I have every confidence that God can similarly sustain you. In fact, He's told us He will! It's our job to fall at His feet in sweet submission to His will. It's His job to equip us with whatever it takes to get us through our trials and bring us into His kingdom.

Why Me?

As Christians, I believe we sometimes forget that we're not exempt from pain and suffering. So when it hits, whether you verbalize the question or not, it's really easy to think, "Why me?" A more appropriate question however might be, "Why not me?"

We really shouldn't be shocked by the suffering and trials that befall us. We're warned about them in the Bible. "Beloved, do not be surprised at the fiery trial when it comes upon you to test you, as though something strange were happening to you" (1 Peter 4:12). It shouldn't seem strange or unfair to us. We should expect it. In fact, Jesus Christ Himself assured us that there will be suffering and trials in our lives. In one of my favorite verses He says, "I have said these things to you, that *in me you may have peace.* In the world you *will* have tribulation. But take heart; *I have overcome the world*" (John 16:33, emphasis added).

Yes, He tells us to expect trouble in this world. But He doesn't leave us there without hope. Instead, in the next sentence He gives us all the hope we need by telling us the victory is already won! He has overcome the world—notice the past tense! Although it hasn't happened yet it is already a "done deal" in the plan of God!

In a way it's like a basketball game. The game has been hard-fought until the last six minutes. Then your favorite team gradually starts pulling together, scoring on every trip down the court. Now there are only 22.4 seconds on the game clock and your team is ahead 88–67! Though you can't *officially* say you've won, you know that in a matter of time, the victory is yours. You start the celebration before the game is even over! That's what we need to do. We can go ahead and start the celebration! As John MacArthur says, "I've read the end of the Book. We win!"[2] In the meantime, the game is not over yet. We will be engaged in this battle until God calls us home, until He (the Coach) puts us on the bench for the rest of the game! Okay, okay, enough of the basketball metaphor. I trust you get my point.

Though Christ has already won our victory, we still live in this world and must deal with the events of our lives, whether we perceive them as good or bad. Though our citizenship is in heaven, we still must focus on living productive lives here on earth in a way that is pleasing to the One who bought us with His blood.

How can we do that when there is so much pain, suffering, misery, and unhappiness in our lives? With a simple but profound response . . . *trust*! Can you truly trust God when the going gets tough? If He's actually in control, then why did He allow your father to have cancer? How could He let such an event as the World Trade Center tragedy occur? Does God actually control all the circumstances in our lives?

Jerry Bridges writes, "I mistakenly thought I could not trust God unless I *felt* like trusting Him (which I almost never did in times of adversity). Now I am learning that *trusting God is first of all a matter of the will, and is not dependent on my feelings*. I choose to trust God and my feelings eventually follow"[3] (emphasis added). Psalm 56:3–4 essentially says the same thing:

> *When I am afraid,*
>   *I put my trust in you.*
> In God, whose word I praise,
>   *in God I trust; I shall not be afraid.*
> What can flesh do to me? (emphasis added)

Remember the promise! "And we know that in all things God works for the good of those who love him, who have been called according to his purpose" (Rom. 8:28 NIV). If we are Christians, we trusted Him with our salvation. Therefore, we can also trust Him with our lives!

An Old Testament equivalent of this verse is found in the account of the life of Joseph. Joseph had been the target of the envy and jealousy of his brothers. They secretly sold him to the Ishmaelites, who took him to Egypt as their slave. The brothers told their father that Joseph had been killed by a wild animal. But Joseph, though he suffered significant hardship, never lost faith in God. Eventually, God worked out the circumstances that led to Joseph's rise in authority in Egypt until he was second only to the king! Years later, he and his brothers were reunited due to circumstances clearly brought about by God. The brothers were afraid that Joseph would have them killed in retaliation for their wickedness in selling him into slavery. But Joseph didn't return evil for evil. He repaid them with love and provision, telling them, " 'As for you, *you meant evil against me, but God meant it for good*, to bring it about that many people should be kept alive, as they are today' " (Gen. 50:20, emphasis added).

Theologian Wayne Grudem writes, "God uses the experience of death to complete our sanctification . . . therefore, we should see all the hardship and suffering that comes to us in life as something that God brings to us to do us good, strengthening our trust in Him and our obedience and ultimately increasing our ability to glorify Him."[4] If you remember anything at all about what I am telling you regarding the purposes of suffering, remember this: *Everything that is brought into our lives is there because God either caused it, or allowed it to be there. And whatever is brought into our lives is designed by God for our best good and for His glory.* You might say to yourself, "Well, I just don't believe that!" And that changes what? Nothing. Truth is just as true whether you believe it or not! However, I hope you will see that what I have said above about the ultimate purposes of suffering is the truth according to the Holy Word of God to His people.

Why should we believe the truth of Scripture? Because God has commanded it. In 2 Timothy 3:16–17, we read, "*All Scripture is breathed out by God* and profitable for teaching, for reproof, for correction, and for training in righteousness, that the man of God may be competent, equipped for every good work" (emphasis added). The authors of the Bible wrote under the direct inspiration of the Holy Spirit. We believe that God, who has authority over all things, has preserved His Word for us to study and obey.

The worship pastor at our church, Todd Murray, wrote a song called "Love Note" to help his children understand about the Bible. He says in his album notes regarding this song, "Written for my children . . . to help them understand that my fatherly love for them is at best a pale reflection of the perfect and infinite love of THE heavenly father." Here is an excerpt from "Love Note":

> Daddy, help me. It's hard to understand
> About the God you say Who loves me
> And Who made me with His hand.
> But God seems so big and heaven far away
> And yet you tell me that He hears me
> When I bow my knees to pray.
> But I can't see God. I can't touch Him.
> I can't hold His hand.
> I can't hear Him talking to me.
> Daddy, I don't understand.
>
> Refrain:
> Just like Daddy leaves a love note on the kitchen table
> Whenever he goes away
> To remind you that I love you,
> And that I'm coming back soon and I want you to obey.
> Well, just like me, your heavenly Father
> Left a letter and every word is true.
> You'll find it written in the pages of the Holy Bible,
> God the Father's love note just for you.

The Bible is God's "love note" to His children but also a strong warning for all mankind! Scripture, like God's love, is something that becomes more beautiful the more in-depth you examine it. The Bible is a treasure chest overflowing with the priceless jewels of truth.

The Purposes of Suffering and Death

When Jesus clearly taught the disciples about His own resurrection, they just didn't get it! They didn't understand (or perhaps didn't even remember) what He'd told them until after it had happened. Even then, they were slow to remember what they had been taught.

Well, we can't be too hard on the disciples. After all, we do the same thing with the subjects of adversity, suffering, and death! These subjects and the purposes of adversity appear throughout the Bible. We are told to expect trials, suffering, death, resurrection, and ultimately eternal life. (We will all have eternal life, but not all will spend it in the same place.) But despite reading it throughout the Scriptures, we seem surprised when adversity and death actually intrude into our lives! You see, we just don't get it either!

To better understand this difficult subject, let's look at the life of the apostle Paul. The Scriptures give few greater examples than Paul; few men could live more devoted and pleasing lives to Christ than he did. Paul was keenly focused on living according to the principles and commands of Jesus Christ and boldly proclaimed them to both Jews and Gentiles. Since he was such a holy and wise man of God, he must have been exceedingly blessed by Him, right? He must have had a pretty happy life! God would just naturally protect someone like that from anything bad that could come his way, wouldn't He? However, looking at Paul's life with this understanding, we might conclude that God didn't like this guy very much. Let's examine some of the events that were placed in Paul's life and see what we think. Was this a blessed life?

In 2 Corinthians 11:23–28, Paul makes a point to the Corinthians, some of whom had cast suspicions on his motives and authority as an apostle. As part of the argument he says,

> I have worked much harder, *been in prison* more frequently, *been flogged* more severely, and *been exposed to death* again and again. *Five times* I received from the Jews the *forty lashes minus one. Three times* I was *beaten with rods,* once I was *stoned, three times* I was *shipwrecked,* I *spent a night and a day in the open sea,* I have been *constantly on the move.* I have been in *danger from rivers,* in *danger from bandits,* in *danger from my own countrymen,* in *danger from Gentiles;* in *danger in the city,* in *danger in*

the country, in *danger at sea;* and in *danger from false brothers.* I have *labored* and *toiled* and have *often gone without sleep;* I have known *hunger* and *thirst* and have *often gone without food;* I have been *cold* and *naked.* Besides everything else, I face *daily* the *pressure of my concern* for all the churches. (NIV, emphasis added)

Quite a life! And this was only the beginning of Paul's ministry. Would we be jealous of such a life? I think not. I sometimes complain if I break a fingernail or have to skip a meal!

But this is the same Paul who several years later said, *"for I have learned to be content whatever the circumstances.* I know what it is to be in need, and I know what it is to have plenty. *I have learned the secret of being content in any and every situation,* whether well fed or hungry, whether living in plenty or in want. I can do everything through him who gives me strength" (Phil. 4:11–13 NIV, emphasis added). Why did Paul have to suffer so? The world might say it was to make him tougher, and that may have been one of the reasons. However, Paul gives another answer:

> For we do not want you to be ignorant, brothers, of the affliction we experienced in Asia. For we were so utterly burdened beyond our strength that we despaired of life itself. Indeed, we felt that we had received the sentence of death. *But that was to make us rely not on ourselves but on God* who raises the dead. He delivered us from such a deadly peril, and he *will* deliver us. *On him we have set our hope* that he will deliver us again. (2 Cor. 1:8–10, emphasis added)

In the Old Testament we're told about God's chosen people, the Jews, and the sufferings they encountered. Later, we're told about David, who is called "a man after God's own heart," and the sufferings brought into his life. The many prophets and priests who belonged to God encountered grief, affliction, and sometimes death, at nearly every turn. In the New Testament John the Baptist, most of Jesus' twelve beloved disciples, the apostle Paul, and some of Jesus' dear friends as well as some of His own family lived lives peppered with suffering. Through the New Testament and subsequent church history we find that most of them were eventually put to death because of their allegiance to Christ.

Jesus Christ Himself lived a life of poverty. A life endangered by the schemes of the Jews, betrayal by one of His disciples, isolation, and slander. He was mocked and beaten by soldiers, flogged, made to carry His own cross to Calvary, and then crucified by having His precious hands and feet nailed to the cross. He was raised naked and bleeding in front of the masses gathered there, bearing intense agony as the cross was lowered with a thud into the ground. Then came the worst part of all. He had to accept the filthiness of the sins of His people, to take them upon Himself, and to die at the hands of men He created, suffering the agony of separation from His Father. What a life! And He was perfect!

Still, we believe that as long as we are "good people" and try to do what's right and go to church and read our Bibles that we should somehow live happy lives. If this kind of shallow happiness was the consequence of our acts of righteousness then that might even be the case. But that's not how God does things. Remember, Christ was perfectly righteous and had the power to give Himself all things, but instead lived His life as the Man of Sorrows. My point is this: if suffering and death were such a huge part of these sanctified lives, why do we feel unfairly treated and betrayed when we don't get our way, or when afflictions befall us, or when we lose loved ones to sickness and death? Shame on us. *We just don't get it!*

The fact is that Christians suffer along with the rest of mankind. We get old and wrinkled. We contract cancer and heart disease. We have accidents or get sick and eventually die. That's part of being alive—the last part! Just as we each have a beginning, we also have an end, and sometimes it's not very pretty. But that shouldn't be surprising. God, our heavenly Father, calls us to serve Him even when we are not in the mood, even when we're not where we want to be, and even when our lives are not easy. In fact, these are especially the times we should call out to Him for the grace to serve Him better.

It is with this understanding that we can then say, like the apostle Paul, "Not that I am speaking of being in need, for I have learned in whatever situation I am to be content" (Phil. 4:11). Once we come to understand this important principle, despair and sadness can be replaced with the quiet, calm assurance that all things rest within God's sovereign control. We can then demonstrate an attitude of confidence and peace knowing that God is working out all things in our lives for our best good, whether we understand how or not. We are to simply trust Him, even when we don't understand.

Jerry Bridges expands this thought about trusting God:

> Trusting God is not a matter of my feelings but of my will. I never feel like trusting God when adversity strikes, but I can choose to do so even when I don't feel like it. That act of the will, though, must be based on belief, and belief must be based on truth.
>
> The truth we must believe is that God is sovereign. He carries out His own good purposes without ever being thwarted, and He so directs and controls all events and all actions of His creatures that they never act outside of His sovereign will. We must believe this and cling to this in the face of adversity and tragedy, if we are to glorify God by trusting Him.
>
> I will say this next statement as gently and compassionately as I know how. Our first priority in times of adversity is to honor and glorify God by trusting Him. We tend to make our first priority the gaining of relief from our feelings of heartache or disappointment or frustration. . . .
>
> The first thing we have to do in order to trust God is determine if God is in control; if He is sovereign over the physical area of our lives. If He is not—if illness and afflictions "just happen"—then, of course, there is no basis for trusting God. But if God is sovereign in this area, then we can trust Him without understanding all the theological issues involved in the problem of pain.[5]

The remainder of this book will look at some of the purposes of suffering. I pray that through this brief study the Holy Spirit will bless our hearts with the understanding we'll need to truly begin to "get it."

Questions for Reflection

1. Based on the verses that began this chapter, what characteristics does suffering produce? Are these characteristics you would like to possess in your life? Why or why not?

2. Apart from God, what other things do suffering people turn to for comfort? Will these things give them true, lasting comfort? What might be the consequences of looking in all the wrong places for a balm for your pain? What is the only true source of comfort?

3. Many Christians tend to respond to painful trials by saying (or thinking), "Why me?" According to this chapter, what might be a more appropriate question?

4. Is it accurate to assume that God will shield us from all adversity as long as we are obedient to His Word and live godly lives? Why or why not? Have you ever been guilty of this kind of thinking?

5. According to Jerry Bridges's quote at the end of the chapter, what should be our first priority in times of adversity? What priority do we tend toward instead? Next time you experience suffering, what will be your priority? To escape from the pain or to honor God through it all?

2

THE ORIGIN OF SUFFERING

So when the woman saw that the tree was good for food, and that it was a delight to the eyes, and that the tree was to be desired to make one wise, she took of its fruit and ate, and she also gave some to her husband who was with her, and he ate. Then the eyes of both were opened, and they knew that they were naked.

—Genesis 3:6–7

Somebody Blew It!

According to Genesis, God placed Adam and Eve in a garden; a beautiful paradise where they could dwell forever in perfect harmony with God. In this perfect, delightful world, there was no sin, no sickness, no sorrow, no suffering, and no death. As husband and wife they lived in complete unity with each other and were placed in a position of dominion over the earth and all the other creatures God had made. Everything was bliss . . . until they blew it.

God gave them one command in relation to the trees in the garden of Eden. Genesis 2:16–17 says, "And the LORD God commanded the man, saying, 'You may surely eat of every tree of the garden, but of the tree of the knowledge of good and evil you shall not eat, for in the day that you eat of it you shall surely die.' " They clearly understood the command. Eve demonstrated her understanding when she clarified the serpent's attempt to distort God's word. He said to her, "Did God actually say, 'You shall not eat of any tree in the garden'?" (Gen. 3:1). Eve immediately replied, "We may eat of the fruit of the trees in the garden, but God said, 'You shall not eat of the fruit of the tree that is in the midst of the garden' " (Gen. 3:2–3). She knew she could eat of the other trees, just not the one in the middle of the garden.

So she obeyed what God commanded, right? Wrong. The serpent convinced her to eat the fruit of this tree and Eve, in turn, convinced her husband to eat it. And in this act of disobedience to God's law, the first sin was committed. Because of Adam's sin of disobedience, where he dishonored and disregarded God's clear command, God levied a curse on *all* mankind—every man, woman, and child who would proceed from this union of first man and woman. That curse ensured that the earth would not remain a paradise and that the fellowship of man and God would be forever ruined.

Adam had walked with God in the garden. He had enjoyed perfect fellowship with Him. There was no chasm between them until Adam's sin. Instead of walking freely with God, they ran from Him. "And they heard the sound of the LORD God walking in the garden in the cool of the day, *and the man and his wife hid themselves from the presence of the LORD God* among the trees of the garden" (Gen. 3:8, emphasis added). They knew they'd blown it! They knew they had disobeyed God's command and already guilt had entered the picture. No longer did they have perfect unity with Him. *Adam's sin, and the resulting curse God placed on Adam and all mankind brought pain, suffering, and death into the world*. That was the origin. Romans 5:12 explains, "Therefore, just as sin came into the world through one man, and death through sin, and so death spread to all men because all sinned."

It is because of that sin that we now have suffering, pain, and death. Our earth experiences chaos as well in the form of hurricanes, earthquakes, volcanoes, tsunamis, and so many other natural disasters. We can see this in Romans 8:19–22. "For the creation waits with eager longing for the revealing of the sons of God. For the creation was subjected to futility, not willingly, but because of him who subjected it, in hope that the creation itself will be set free from its bondage to decay and obtain the freedom of the glory of the children of God. For we know that the whole creation has been groaning together in the pains of childbirth until now." No more do we have a perfect paradise. No more can we enjoy a relationship with our Father free from sin. Adam's act of rebellion is what caused the chasm that has existed between God and man ever since. *That sin is the first of many that made it necessary to have a way across that chasm, and the only way across is through the substitutionary righteousness of Jesus Christ, the Son of God.*

God, the Father, made a way for His children to come to Him and to reign with Him forever. Will all men, women, and children find the way across? No. We're told in Matthew 7:13, "Enter by the narrow gate. For the gate is wide and the way is easy that leads to destruction, and those who enter by it are *many*. For the gate is narrow and the way is hard that leads to life, and those who find it are *few*" (emphasis added). Are we to understand that we are to somehow find this narrow gate on our own, stumbling around until we discover it? No, not at all. God not only made provision for there to be a "gate" leading to eternal life with Him, but also enables His children to find it. Jesus tells us in John 14:6, "I am the way, and the truth, and the life. No *one comes to the Father except through me*" (emphasis added).

Therefore, even though man brought upon himself the dark things of this life (sickness, sin, suffering, and death), God, in His sovereign mercy, demonstrated His grace by providing salvation for His children. Yes, He brings suffering into our lives now, but He also equips us with the tools we need to get through such suffering and persevere until the end.

Perhaps you've heard the saying, "If God brings us to it, He'll bring us through it."

To Explain It Another Way

We've already talked about the *origin* of suffering. Now let's discuss the *reasons* for it.

There are at least two main reasons that suffering exists in the world. Primarily, it exists because God decreed it. Secondly, suffering fits within God's plan for His creation. Nothing happens that is not either caused or allowed by Him. What function does it have in His plan? Ultimately, suffering exists to accomplish God's purposes.

Though it is my desire to offer comfort through a better understanding of some of the reasons behind our own suffering and grief, my ultimate goal is to glorify God's greatness in the workings of His perfect will. His thoughts are above our thoughts. "For as the heavens are higher than the earth, so are my ways higher than your ways and my thoughts than your thoughts" (Isa. 55:9). The mind of God is so awesome that no one will ever be able to thoroughly comprehend the reasons for what He does. "Oh, the depth of the *riches* and *wisdom* and *knowledge* of God! How unsearchable are his judgments and how inscrutable his ways! 'For who has known the mind of the Lord, or who has been his counselor? Or who has given a gift to him that he might be repaid?' For *from* him and *through* him and *to* him are *all things. To him be glory forever.* Amen" (Rom. 11:33–36, emphasis added).

As I've mentioned above, with such a transcendent God as this, the bottom line for suffering is because God decreed it. Perhaps you remember when your parents used to say, "Because I said so!" When I was young, I told myself I'd never give that answer to my children. I hated it when my mother said it to me. Imagine my surprise when years later I found myself telling my children "because I said so!" It wasn't until I had children that I realized it is sometimes the most appropriate answer! I finally understood how important the concept of authority was.

Parents have a God-given authority over children. Children must recognize that authority and submit to it if order and discipline are to be maintained in the home. It gives them a model (however imperfect) of our own submission to God. When children question your authority there are times you must remind them that the bottom line for their obedience is "because I said so." There are other times when reasoning with them may be appropriate and, in fact, advisable. But "because I said so" demonstrates who is in control. Not the child, but the parent. Not the creature but the Creator.

God is under no obligation to us for anything. He is like the artist wielding the brush, like the potter shaping the clay, like the architect drawing the design. God is the ultimate "artist" of our very being—body and soul! He can do what He wants. He doesn't owe us any explanations! "He does according to his will among the host of heaven and among the inhabitants of the earth; and none can stay his hand or say to him, 'What have you done?' " (Dan. 4:35).

In the following passage, Paul anticipates the question his readers might ask to this declaration of God's sovereignty. "That's not fair!" they might whine. So Paul addresses the "fairness" of the situation by telling them that God is God. He can do whatever He wants to do. And He has the power and authority to back it up! Romans 9:20–21 says, "But who are you, O man, to answer back to God? Will *what is molded* say to its *molder*, 'Why have you made me like this?' Has the potter no right over the clay, to make out of the same lump one vessel for honored use and another for dishonorable use?" (emphasis added).

As Jerry Bridges writes,

God's sovereignty involves *His absolute power* to do whatever pleases Him and *His absolute control* over the actions of all His creatures. But God's sovereignty also includes *His absolute right* to do as He pleases with us. That He has chosen to redeem us and to send His Son to die for us, instead of sending us to Hell, is not due to any *obligation* toward us on His part. It is solely due to His *sovereign mercy and grace*. As He said to Moses, "I will have mercy on whom I will have mercy and I will have compassion on whom I will have compassion" (Exodus 33:19). By that statement God was saying, "I am under obligation to no one"[1] (emphasis added).

Bottom line, that's the reason suffering and death exist in this world—because God said so! He decreed them to be. Suffering, hardships and death must not be interpreted as evidence of God's supposed lack of fairness. Instead, it should be regarded as His well-considered sentence against sin.

The age-old problem some people have in making sense of suffering and pain is that they may think God is either totally good but not all-powerful, or that He is all-powerful but not totally good. They have a tough time reconciling God's goodness and His power. Fortunately we are not forced to choose between the sovereignty and the goodness of God. God is both— all-powerful and totally and completely good. His sovereignty and His goodness are both asserted in the Bible with equal emphasis. References to His goodness and loving-kindness, as well as His sovereignty, appear on almost every page.

Suffering exists because it fits within God's plan for His creation. It serves to accomplish His purposes. Throughout the Bible, in both the Old and New Testaments, we're given examples of God using suffering or death to do just this. One such example is in Hebrews 2:14–15 where we read, "Since therefore the children share in flesh and blood, he himself [Christ] likewise partook of the same things, that through death he might destroy the one who has the power of death, that is, the devil, and deliver all those who *through fear of death* were subject to *lifelong slavery*" (emphasis added). Christ's own suffering and death accomplished His purposes in defeating Satan and in redeeming the children of God, freeing them from their fear of death. "I cry out to God Most High, to God who fulfills his purpose for me" (Ps. 57:2). He *always* achieves the desired outcome! "And he is not served by human hands, as if he needed anything, because *he himself gives all men life and breath and everything else*. From one man he made every nation of men, that they should inhabit the whole earth; and *he determined the times set for them and the exact places where they should live* . . . 'For *in him*, we *live* and *move* and *have our being*' " (Acts 17:25–26, 28 NIV, emphasis added). If this is not a divine Master Planner, I don't know what is!

Moving to John 9 we see Christ healing a man who had been blind from birth. In that day, sickness was frequently attributed to sin. That prompted the following question (and Christ's answer): "And his disciples asked him, 'Rabbi [Teacher], who sinned, this man or his parents, that he was born blind?' Jesus answered, 'It was not that this man sinned, or his parents, but *that the works of God might be displayed in him*' " (John 9:2–3, emphasis added). In this case, God's purposes were accomplished through suffering. The man's sight was given to him and God received the glory.

It should be enough for God to tell His poor, sinful children that suffering exists in this world to accomplish His purposes. But He is a merciful God who loves us enough to provide more specific answers to this perplexing question. We'll discuss a few of them in the following chapters.

Questions for Reflection

1. What was the big deal about eating a piece of fruit? Why did Adam's sin affect the rest of us?

2. According to Genesis, what was the first clue that things had changed after Adam and Eve sinned against God?
3. Do we have the ability on our own to cross the enormous chasm that exists between God and man? God provided His children with a way across the chasm. Explain. Could you articulate this concept clearly to another person? If so, then do it! If you can't explain it to someone else, then work on it until you can! Then do it! That's the gospel—and we are to share it, not keep it to ourselves.
4. Do you ever act with childish rebellion toward the circumstances God brings into your life? What underlying principle should you remember during times like this? What things fall under God's authority?
5. According to John 9, why was the man born blind? In light of this, what reason do you think underlies our own suffering? Are you mindful of that fact when you suffer? During these hard times, do you ever stop to consider how you may honor and glorify God through your trials?

Purposes Common to All Suffering

3

TO COMPLETE OUR SANCTIFICATION

Count it all joy, my brothers, when you meet trials of various kinds, for you know that the testing of your faith produces steadfastness. And let steadfastness have its full effect, *that you may be perfect and complete, lacking in nothing.*

—James 1:2–4 (emphasis added)

Suffering Leads to Spiritual Maturity

"Do not be conformed to this world, but be *transformed* by the *renewal of your mind*, that by testing you may discern what is the will of God, what is good and acceptable and perfect" (Rom. 12:2, emphasis added). After we become believers our hearts and our minds gradually become transformed through what we learn about our Lord from the Scriptures! We start to become more like Christ.

As one of my teachers explains, when we spend a great deal of time with someone, we naturally begin to take on some of his or her traits. Perhaps we take on certain phrases they use or inflections in their speech, or distinct characteristics or gestures. In this same way, when we spend more and more time with Christ through prayer and study we begin to take on some of *His* characteristics. In other words, we become increasingly Christlike as we spend time with Him. As we grow spiritually we seek to understand what we need to do to live lives pleasing to Christ. The more we understand the word of God in the Bible, the more we undergo this transformation in our minds and hearts. This ongoing transformation of becoming more like Christ is called sanctification. Sanctification means that we are being set apart for a specific purpose. In this case, we are set apart to glorify God.

Salvation, or justification, occurs in a moment of time. It occurs the instant you place your trust in Christ as your Savior and Lord. One is just as "saved" at that moment as someone who was saved forty years ago. It happens in a moment and remains constant forever. But sanctification is an ongoing process. It is gradual and progressive. We are to grow in our Christlikeness for the rest of our lives, though we will never attain such perfection on this side of death. His standard is the one we strive for but cannot fully achieve in this life.

The Master's Tools

What tools does God use to transform us into the people He wants us to be? He knows exactly what circumstances, both good and bad, are necessary to produce the desired result in us. He uses the events in our lives, the gifts He gives us, the people with whom we come into contact, and most of all, He uses His word to us in the Scriptures. His tools are limitless. Imagine for a moment that we are blocks of marble. God precisely chisels everything around us until we are finally the image He wants us to be. The tools work through chipping, pummeling, scraping away, and pounding into shape, removing the useless or meaningless spall from around us.

Sometimes that's what it feels like when trials and disappointments come our way. We feel the pain and discomfort and can be so focused on the *feeling* that we don't recognize the good it's bringing forth. God brings circumstances into our lives. That's true whether we're believers or unbelievers. But He's made a promise to believers. "And we know that in all things God works for the good of those who love him, who have been called according to his purpose" (Rom. 8:28 NIV, emphasis added). *What exactly is included in "all things"? Well, that would be . . . everything! Do adversity, suffering, grief, disappointment, sickness and even death fall into that category? Absolutely!* Do we have to understand what God is doing and what His ultimate goal is for our lives before we can trust in that promise? By no means!

Our worship pastor, Todd Murray, has composed many beautiful Christian songs. One of my favorites is "I Am Not Alone." The lyrics are words of comfort and conviction. Here is a portion of it:

> I will not resist You, *when You move Your hand to mold me.*
> I will not *insist* You show me all Your plans today.
> *I will not despise the tools You're using now to shape me.*
> I will not require *understanding* to *obey.*
> And I refuse to fear, when the future is unclear,
> Knowing You are here close beside me.
> *When I haven't got a clue, what it is that You're up to,*
> *Even then I know that You have not abandoned me.*
> 'Cause faith is believing in things that are yet unseen.
> Faith is believing God will intervene. (emphasis added)

His tools are sometimes tools that chip away, change us, and mold our thinking, our behavior, our attitudes, and even our lifestyles. God uses these tools to make us better, that is, to make us more like Him. Sometimes the tools He uses are suffering and adversity. Again, Jerry Bridges beautifully sums up this truth:

There is no question that adversity is difficult. It usually takes us by surprise and seems to strike where we are most vulnerable. To us it often appears completely senseless and irrational, but to God none of it is either senseless or irrational. He has a purpose in every pain He brings or allows in our lives. We can be sure that in some way He intends it for our profit and His glory.[1]

The Blessings of Hardship

Jeremiah 29:11 says, " 'For I know the plans I have for you, declares the LORD, plans for *wholeness* and *not for evil, to give you a future and a hope*' " (emphasis added). In years past I've wondered how certain circumstances in my life could possibly work to my good. For example, there was the time when I was a single mom with two little boys to support. Finances were almost impossibly tight and we really had to struggle to get by. I couldn't even pay for two haircuts out of the same paycheck. I had to do them one at a time. How could that period of my life possibly work to my good? It was hard, but looking back I can see multiple benefits from being poor and working so hard to make ends meet. Here are a few:

Those days were some of the best I've ever had. The closeness of the relationship with my boys was something I'll treasure forever. We didn't have money to do fancy things or to go to expensive places. Our financial situation forced me to think creatively about finding free opportunities to experience joy and togetherness. We spent a lot of time in parks and museums, or having little picnics, or finding a sandy place where they could build castles, or looking up at the stars at night. I taught them to play tennis and throw a football, to catch and hit a baseball. We had races and invented competitions. We visited with friends and family. We went for walks or had sword fights with empty wrapping paper tubes. At the time, I felt sorry for them, wishing I could give them more. But looking back at those times, I am so thankful. My boys didn't miss all the extras. They had what some kids never get—wonderful family times and memories of being very loved.

Being that poor gave me a frame of reference and an appreciation I wouldn't have had otherwise. Sometimes when things are a little tight financially my husband tends to worry. He's never had the blessing of poverty! He doesn't have that frame of reference. It has given me the opportunity to offer him encouragement and reassurance.

Because of my own experiences, I've been better able to empathize with others. I can never look down on those less fortunate. I know firsthand what some of these people are going through. What a blessing that has been.

I was reminded many times of God's providence and mercy to me, and His utter goodness and grace to provide for His children. On paper, it didn't look like I'd be able to make all my payments every month. Yet I did! Something always happened to make it possible. Good luck, perhaps? Not at all. Instead, it was a gracious God! For instance, He placed people in my life who helped make it possible—the sweet old man who owned the neighborhood grocery store, my mother who taught me how to budget, my friends, my pastor, and a few of my neighbors. They knew how tough things were for me. They helped me so much. I know those people were placed in my life by a loving God. He was not punishing me by making me poor. He was blessing me! It just didn't seem like it at the time.

There are other examples I could use to demonstrate how the trials God gave me worked out for my good. Eventually I came to realize this. After a while, I started to remember that fact *during* a crisis. Now I know *in advance* that whatever He brings into my life is brought about for a reason that will ultimately be for my good and will make me better in the process.

He has delivered me so many times. He has a proven track record, and He never fails in His purposes.

These experiences have only served to strengthen my trust and faith in Him. I know I am the person I am today because of the lifetime of experiences He has given me. And it's not over yet. He's still blessing me and changing me. I'm a work in progress and so are you. As we grow in maturity, we seek to become more like Christ. Galatians 2:19–20 says, "I have been crucified with Christ. It is no longer I who live, but Christ who lives in me." Can you say that? Only God can bring us to that point in Christian maturity. Doug Reed, pastor at Thorncrown Chapel in Eureka Springs, Arkansas, wrote about this verse saying, "Two of the great tools God uses to bring us to this realization are our sufferings and our failures . . . so, let us press on to maturity knowing full well its definition: *more* of Christ and *less* of us"[2] (emphasis added).

Examples of Godliness

Who comes to mind when you consider people who demonstrate godliness through suffering? The apostle Paul? Job? King David? John the Baptist? Someone you know personally? What gives them the ability to glorify God through their suffering? Were they just stronger than we are? Do we have more fragile temperaments? Did they not have to suffer as much as we do? No. It didn't depend on their own strength! It was the Lord's strength that saw them through. How could they do it when it seems we can't? It's that their focus was where it belongs, while ours so often strays. Those great biblical saints, examples to us even now, realized that ultimately *it was all about God. It wasn't about them!* That's what we have to remember. It's not about us. It's *all* about God.

Why doesn't He just take us out of this world when we're saved? Wouldn't that be to His advantage so we can dwell with Him, worshiping and praising Him forever? Yet, He chooses to leave us here on this earth. Why? So we can have happy, fulfilled lives? Did He redeem us with His Son's precious blood so that we can live a trouble-free existence? No. He left us here to serve Him. We're His slaves. The chief purpose of a slave is to serve and please his master. That's what we are to do. As slaves of Christ, we are to have a single focus: to live lives pleasing to Him. Sometimes we lose sight of that and seek to serve our own lusts and desires instead. We want what pleases us instead of what pleases Him. That's why it's so important to make sure our focus is Godward and not selfward. Looking at our lives through a spiritual lens instead of a worldly one will change the way we view the circumstances we resist so fiercely. We are to serve Him through the way we live, think and even feel.

Don't despise the tools He uses to make you better. It has been said that God never puts too much of the salt of adversity into the recipe of our lives. His blend of adversity and blessing is always exactly right for us. Romans 5:3–5 says, "We rejoice in our sufferings, knowing that suffering produces *endurance*, and endurance produces *character*, and character produces *hope*, and hope does not put us to shame, because God's love has been poured into our hearts through the Holy Spirit who has been given to us" (emphasis added). Rejoice in our sufferings? Hah! Only a masochist would do that, you might say.

That's not what the Bible is talking about in this passage. When we're told to rejoice in our sufferings it is for the *benefit* they bring that we rejoice. It is also because we realize this benefit is the gift of God for our lives, whether we understand it or not. He does not ask us to rejoice because a loved one has been stricken with cancer, or because we have lost our job, or because we have constant pain. But we can rejoice because He has assured us that He is in control of all our circumstances and we know they will ultimately work for our good. Remember, we cannot be completely mature without perseverance and we can't obtain the characteristic of perseverance without facing trials. *It is that spiritual maturity that will get us through every trial and every adversity without despair, knowing that our loving Lord holds us safely in the palm of His hand.*

This truth regarding perseverance can be likened to the preparation an athlete makes in order to compete in his or her field of endeavor. Think of the hours of training, the conditioning, the investment in time and energy, and the struggle of sweat and tears they must go through to achieve a level of excellence in their sport. Why do they do it? Because they love it. They understand that the end result is worth all the pain involved in getting there. The phrase "No pain, no gain" applies to our spiritual lives as well. If we are to endure to the end, we have to build endurance, and the only way to build endurance is to endure.

I am reminded of something I've read in several sources regarding the subject of how suffering increases our growth and maturity. The example used is called a Cecropia moth. Jerry Bridges tells about it in *Trusting God*:

> One of the many fascinating events in nature is the emergence of the Cecropia moth from its cocoon—an event that occurs only with much struggle on the part of the moth to free itself. The story is frequently told of someone who watched a moth go through this struggle. In an effort to help—and not realizing the necessity of the struggle—the viewer snipped the shell of the cocoon. Soon the moth came out with its wings all crimped and shriveled. But as the person watched, the wings remained weak. The moth, which in a few moments would have stretched those wings to fly, was now doomed to crawling out its brief life in frustration of ever being the beautiful creature God created it to be.
>
> What the person in the story did not realize was that the struggle to emerge from the cocoon was an essential part of developing the muscle system of the moth's body and pushing the body fluids out into the wings to expand them. By unwisely seeking to cut short the moth's struggle, the watcher had actually crippled the moth and doomed its existence.

The adversities of life are much like the cocoon of the Cecropia moth. God uses them to develop the spiritual 'muscle system' of our lives. . . We can be sure that the development of a beautiful Christlike character will not occur in our lives without adversity.[3]

When my oldest son started walking, I used to take him outside to play. Where the sidewalk met the grass, he always fell. To protect him, I started helping him from one surface to the other. Soon I realized that unless I allowed him to figure this out, he would continue to need my help at that junction every time. So I stood back and let him fall a few times. The tumble into the grass didn't hurt him and after a couple of falls, he began to adjust to the different surfaces and could easily go from one to the other without my assistance.

When God takes us through difficulties, He makes us better, stronger, and smarter than we would be without them. We emerge through them as changed individuals. The more mature our faith is, the more positive and constructive the interpretation of our painful experience becomes. We should learn to appreciate our adversities in advance for the good God will bring about by their use.

Questions for Reflection

1. What is the difference between justification and sanctification?
2. According to this chapter, in what way are we like blocks of marble? What tools does God use to make us who and what He wants us to be? What purpose of suffering does this chapter offer?
3. Can you remember a particularly difficult period in your life that ended up making you stronger, happier, wiser, or more mature? Looking back, can you see God's hand in

those events? Make a list of blessings brought about by tough times.

4. When you experience hardship, do you rely on your own strength? How's that working out for you? Next time God sends you through suffering, will you seek to tap in to His strength to see you through? How do you think that outcome would compare to times when you put your faith in your own abilities?

5. Is it possible to rejoice in our sufferings? Why or why not?

TO DRIVE OUR SOULS TO GOD

For we do not want you to be ignorant, brothers, of the affliction we experienced in Asia. For we were so utterly burdened beyond our strength that we despaired of life itself. Indeed, we felt that we had received the sentence of death. *But that was to make us rely not on ourselves but on God who raises the dead.* He delivered us from such a deadly peril, and he will deliver us. On him we have set our hope that he will deliver us again.

—2 Corinthians 1:8–10 (emphasis added)

Who's in Control?

One of the by-products of trial is that we begin to sense our utter helplessness and inability to change the events of our lives. We begin to realize there is something, or Someone, more powerful than we are and in control of all of life's circumstances.

For the unbeliever that thing in control is chance, fate, or luck. They might think their lives are subject to a toss of the dice or the flip of a coin. Even believers, who don't understand how

God works in their lives, sometimes choose to substitute the doctrine of chance for the doctrine of divine providence. Yet God is sovereign over everyone's life whether they acknowledge it or not. We don't use the term "providence" much anymore. What does it mean? Perhaps the word is better understood as "provide-ence." God's providence is His tireless attendance to our needs. (Of course, the concept of the providence of God is much broader in scope than only this aspect.) Everything we have comes from Him. He provides for us, cares for us, and lovingly rules over us for His own glory and the good of His people.

Christian believers should not believe that fate, chance, or anything else apart from God controls their lives. They must know that God is in control. Often we lose sight of that. Sometimes, especially when things are going our way, it's tempting to start believing that *we* are in control. It is easy to see ourselves as masters of our own destiny or captains of our own souls. How long can we carelessly glide through life that way? Until we are brought face to face with a situation which is *definitely, obviously* out of our control. Then we tardily remember, "Oh yeah. That's within God's control, not mine. I can't do anything about this but He can." It is then that we fall to our knees in prayer, begging God to help us and to forgive our arrogance. And ironically, it is then that we are our strongest because we acknowledge God as our only true source of strength. There is no strength mightier than His. "For the sake of Christ, then, I am content with weaknesses, insults, hardships, persecutions, and calamities. For when I am weak, then I am strong" (2 Cor. 12:10). Doug Reed reiterates this idea in his thesis on spiritual maturity:

> Those, like [the apostle] Paul, who have been through many trials soon begin to realize that tribulation has a much greater purpose than to make us stronger. On the contrary, the Lord at times allows us to be 'burdened beyond our strength' that we might find Him as our strength. *Suffering does not make us good.*

56

It leads us to the place where we find Christ as our good. It brings us to the end of ourselves that we might reach the beginning of God. Often, it is in the midst of our greatest weakness that we learn to be strong in the Lord and in our greatest failure that we find the Lord as our good.[1] (emphasis added)

Sorrow Points Us to God

Sometimes we need to be brought low so we can begin to see God as our strength. I'm reminded of a passage in Lamentations. The period described here is one of the darkest periods in the whole Bible. Although there are lamentations recorded in other books, this is the only book completely devoted to them. Jeremiah finds himself amid the ashes and rubble that once was mighty Jerusalem and cries, "My soul is bereft of peace; I have forgotten what happiness is; so I say, 'My endurance has perished; so has my hope from the LORD.' Remember my affliction and my wanderings, the wormwood and the gall! My soul continually remembers it and is bowed down within me" (Lam. 3:17–20). This is an apt description of what we might call depression today. He has reached the place of hopelessness, but he doesn't stay there. Let's see what causes him to be lifted from this place of despair. Jeremiah continues,

> But this I call to mind,
> and therefore I have hope:
>
> The steadfast love of the LORD never ceases;
> his mercies never come to an end;
> they are new every morning;
> great is your faithfulness.
> "The LORD is my portion," says my soul,
> "therefore I will hope in him."
>
> The LORD is good to those who wait for him,
> to the soul who seeks him.

It is good that one should wait quietly
　　for the salvation of the LORD . . .

For the Lord will not
　　cast off forever,
but, though he cause grief, he will have compassion
　　according to the abundance of his steadfast love. (Lam.
　　　　3:21–26, 31–32)

Jeremiah could have sat there dwelling on his misery for the rest of his life, but he didn't. What was it that brought hope back into his heart? It was meditating on God's steadfast love and compassion. It was by remembering that God's mercies are new every morning and knowing that He would not leave His people in ruins forever. Out of his hopelessness arose hope because of the grace of God. That same hope is available to us!

God made us strong. Psalm 139:13–14 says,

For you formed my inward parts;
　　you knitted me together in my mother's womb.
I praise you, for *I am fearfully and wonderfully made*. (emphasis added)

Our robust bodies were built with the most amazing design imaginable. They can withstand tremendous assault and still repair themselves over and over. Our minds have amazing resilience as well. He blessed us with body and mind that can somehow bear the pain and sorrow of the tragedies we encounter. At the same time, we realize we are merely vessels of clay. We break down, wrinkle, and get sick. Our minds can become frazzled and confused, and ultimately we die. There is no mystery there. Why should it surprise us when we get sick? This is the way of things ever since the fall of Adam. This is just life! Isaiah 40:6–8 says it like this,

A voice says, "Cry!"
　　And I said, "What shall I cry?"

> All flesh is grass,
>> and all its beauty is like the flower of the field.
> The grass withers, the flower fades
>> when the breath of the LORD blows on it;
>> surely the people are grass.
> The grass withers, the flower fades,
>> but the word of our God will stand forever.

The author of Ecclesiastes describes the aging process poetically in Ecclesiastes 12:1–7:

> Remember also your Creator in the days of your youth, before the evil days come and the years draw near of which you will say, 'I have no pleasure in them' before the sun and the light and the moon and the stars are darkened and the clouds return after the rain, in the day when the keepers of the house tremble, and the strong men are bent [their backs], and the grinders [teeth] cease because they are few, and those who look through the windows [eyes] are dimmed, and the doors on the streets are shut—when the sound of the grinding is low [hearing], and one rises up at the sound of a bird, and all the daughters of song are brought low . . . and desire fails, because man is going to his eternal home, and the mourners go about the streets . . . and the dust returns to the earth as it was, and the spirit returns to God who gave it.

We Place Our Hand in His

God is Creator of all things, giver of life, and Sovereign Ruler of our universe. The times of our lives are determined by Him, and so are our circumstances. However, He gives us a body and a mind that can hold up under incredible stress. He takes us by the hand and leads us along our journey through life. He upholds us with His strong right hand:

> My soul will be satisfied as with fat and rich food,
>> and my mouth will praise you with joyful lips,

> when I remember you upon my bed,
>   and meditate on you in the watches of the night;
> for you have been my help,
>   and in the shadow of your wings I will sing for joy.
> My soul clings to you;
>   your right hand upholds me. (Ps. 63:5–8)

This is a God who loves His children. He has redeemed us with the blood of Christ. He doesn't promise that we'll live trouble-free lives. Instead, He promises that He will walk with us through every trial. 1 Peter 1:3–5 says, "Praise be to the God and Father of our Lord Jesus Christ! In his great mercy he has given us new birth into a living hope through the resurrection of Jesus Christ from the dead, and into an inheritance that can never perish, spoil or fade—kept in heaven for you, who through faith are *shielded by God's power* until the coming of the salvation that is ready to be revealed in the last time" (NIV, emphasis added). Imagine that! We are shielded by God's power. Therefore, do not be afraid. When you find the end of yourself, dry your eyes and lift them heavenward. You'll find God surrounding you with strength and hope and comfort. Through faith, He shields us by His power. What an encouraging truth!

Over a hundred years ago, J. C. Ryle wrote in his commentary on the Gospels:

> There is nothing which shows our ignorance so much as our impatience under trouble. We forget that every cross is a message from God, and intended to do us good in the end. *Trials are intended to make us think—to wean us from the world—to send us to the Bible—to drive us to our knees. Health is a good thing but sickness is far better if it leads us to God. Prosperity is a great mercy; but adversity is a greater one if it brings us to Christ.* Anything, anything is better than living in carelessness and dying in sin[2] (emphasis added).

Questions for Reflection

1. What do unbelievers tend to believe controls their lives? What about Christians? Are we all governed by a toss of the dice, by good or bad luck? What do you think about this?

2. According to this chapter, what might be one benefit derived from the trials and hardships God gives us? Are we more likely to drop to our knees in response to happy times or trying ones?

3. We love to think of ourselves as strong! According to 2 Corinthians 12:10, when are we the strongest?

4. Why do you think we sometimes begin to doubt the Lord's kindness when we're handed a troubling diagnosis? Instead of doubting Him, what should we do/remember?

5. What reason do we have for resisting the urge to be afraid when dark times come? Visualize God as your shield. Will that visualization help you the next time you encounter a fiery trial?

5

TO TEACH US TO TRUST
GOD'S PROMISES

So when God desired to show more convincingly to the
heirs of the promise the unchangeable character of his
purpose, he guaranteed it with an oath, so that by two
unchangeable things, in which *it is impossible for God to
lie*, we who have fled for refuge might have strong encouragement *to hold fast to the hope set before us. We have
this as a sure and steadfast anchor of the soul* . . .

—Hebrews 6:17–19 (emphasis added)

Is God Really Worthy of Our Trust?

You might remember a time as a child standing by the side
of a swimming pool or on a dock over the water. Your father waited in the water, holding his arms out to you, saying, "Jump! I'll catch you!" Perhaps you were terrified the first
time you did it. Would he really catch you? Would you sink
to the bottom and die? Would you get water up your nose?
But you finally mustered all the courage your little heart pos-

sessed and you leapt out over the water into your father's waiting arms. Mission accomplished! The next time, you were less frightened to jump. You knew your father caught you before and that he could do it again! So you jumped again. He caught you again. You shrieked with laughter as you climbed out of the water to do it over and over. Before long, there was no fear at all, but only the trust and assurance that your dad would catch you. What once brought you fear now brought you unimaginable joy!

That's a mere shadow of the kind of trust we can have in God, our heavenly Father. The first time we take a leap of faith into His arms, we may be terrified. Will He really be there for us? The next time, you know He'll keep you from falling because He did it before, because He says He will, and because He does not lie. After several such leaps you begin to recognize the utter reliability of God. Though adversity makes it necessary for you to jump, your heart can rejoice in the faithfulness and loving-kindness of your Father who is waiting there to catch you. "Cast your burden on the LORD, and *he will sustain you*; he will *never* permit the righteous to be moved [fall]" (Ps. 55:22, emphasis added).

A relationship of trust and faith develops in this way. God assures us in the Scriptures that we can place our trust in Him. He tenderly cares for us, and this is promised in Isaiah 40:11, "He [God] will tend his flock like a shepherd; he will gather the lambs in his arms; he will carry them in his bosom, and gently lead those that are with young." We are His lambs if we believe in Christ, the Great Shepherd. It would do us well to undertake a study of the promises of God. Look them up and write them down on index cards. Meditate on these promises and pray for a heart that trusts in them. Perhaps you'll want to carry the cards around with you so you'll have them available during the hard times—sitting in a waiting room anticipating a diagnosis from the doctor, having coffee with a friend in need, or waiting for a tow truck to pick up your newly wrecked car. Make positive use of the time spent waiting in line at the grocery store, at a red light, or before church to prepare your heart for worship. Memorize as many of them as you can so they'll be readily available to you when you need them most.

It has been said that God never promised us smooth sailing. Instead, He promised us safe harbor. When we study His promises, we learn that this is true. Such a study is more than an epistemological exercise. It is an activity that will provide great dividends in relation to our state of mind and heart during challenging times. *When we saturate our minds with the promises of God, we teach ourselves how to think in a God-honoring, trusting way. It pleases Him when we rely on Him for our every concern.* When we're facing hardship, suffering, calamity, our own death, or the death of a loved one, can we still trust in the promises of God? Absolutely! The more hurtful the trial the more we can rely on His faithfulness to us. In *Dying Thoughts*, Richard Baxter, when facing his own impending death, wrote, "Never did God break his promise with me. Never did he fail me, or forsake me. And shall I now distrust him at last?"[1] His answer was no. We can trust our God in everything!

One of my dear friends had to undergo a difficult surgery a few years ago. There were times when the doctors didn't hold out much hope for him to live. It was certainly not a pleasant experience for him to be that close to death, but he reassured many of his friends and family that he was relying totally on the sovereignty of God for his life and asked them to do so as well. If God chose to take him, he was ready, and if He chose to leave him here longer, he was appreciative of that as well. He demonstrated a steadfast faith and trust in our almighty Father. As it turned out, it pleased God to make the surgery successful and to allow him to spend additional time with us here.

But along with the discomfort, the suffering, and the apprehension of this experience, my friend experienced numerous gestures of love and support from his friends, family, our church body, and the pastoral staff. He was amazed by all this attention. He knew he had many, many friends, but it took this experience to demonstrate to him the depth of our caring. In the midst of this adversity he experienced some delightful manifestations of God's love for him. Consider the words of David in Psalm 145:13–21:

> The LORD *is faithful in all his words*
>   and kind in all his works.
> The LORD upholds all who are falling
>   and raises up all who are bowed down.
> The eyes of all look to you,
>   and you give them their food *in due season.*
> You open your hand;
>   you satisfy the desire of every living thing.
> The LORD is righteous in all his ways
>   and kind in all his works.
> The LORD *is near to all who call on him,*
>   *to all who call on him in truth.*
> He fulfills the desire *of those who fear him;*
>   he also hears their cry and saves them.
> The LORD preserves *all who love him,*
>   but all the wicked he will destroy.
> My mouth will speak the praise of the LORD,
>   and *let all flesh bless his holy name forever and ever.*
>   (emphasis added)

God does not promise that we will never have sorrow or tribulation. He guarantees that we will! Nothing and no one is out of God's reach. There is nothing permanent on this earth. He can take unto Himself anything that we love, and it is His sovereign right to do so. But as the psalmist points out above, God, our Father, upholds us when we're falling. He raises us up when we are bowed down. He gives us what we need exactly when we need it.

There is one thing that cannot change, cannot diminish, cannot disappoint, and cannot be taken from us. That is the love of God. Anything else in our lives must take second place to Him. That abiding love is there through any trial and will be there even if everything you love is taken away. That one constant is why you can live through any loss, any pain, any sorrow, or any hardship.

Questions for Reflection

1. According to the Hebrews 6 passage with which I began this chapter, what is one of the main reasons we can trust what God says?

2. Can you remember a time where you recognized God's faithfulness in your life? What were the circumstances? If He has such a proven track record with each of us, why do you think we still get scared when faced with situations beyond our control?

3. Is Jesus Christ really your Great Shepherd? Do you follow where He leads? Is your submission willing or resentful?

4. According to this chapter, "It has been said that God never promised us _____ _____. Instead, He promised us ____ _____." What does this mean to you?

5. How can we teach ourselves to think in God-honoring, trusting ways? Why would that please Him?

6

TO PREPARE US
FOR COMING GLORY

Blessed is the man who remains steadfast under trial, for
when he has stood the test he will receive the *crown of
life*, which God has promised to those who love him.
—James 1:12 (emphasis added)

Focus on the Eternal, Not the Temporal

Occasionally you might read a sign that asks, "Are you living
your life with the end in mind?" I used to think such signs
were a little morbid, and if you interpret "the end" as death,
I suppose they are. But death isn't really the end, is it? It's
merely a line of demarcation.

Charles Spurgeon, one of the nineteenth century's most
brilliant preachers, said, "Think not that heaven and earth are
divided. They are but kindred worlds, two ships moored close
to one another, one short plank of death will enable you to
step from one into the other."[1] Eternity awaits us on the other
side. For believers in Jesus Christ, that eternity will be joyfully

spent in the presence of our King. It is that end that we are to keep in mind as we live our lives.

My work as a hospice nurse for over a decade has allowed me to witness many times the precious moment when a person takes that ultimate step from this life into the next. No matter how often I see it, it never loses its poignancy, and it is never taken lightly. And though all of us are destined to die, unless Christ comes back in the meantime, we shouldn't be morbidly fascinated with death, but instead we should have an eternal view of what lies beyond it.

We must live our lives with an eternal perspective. What do I mean by that? We have a tendency to focus on our present troubles and find it difficult to see beyond them. In earlier chapters, I've asserted that there will be an eventual beneficial result from our sufferings. The sufferings are now. Many times, the blessing comes later. So the Scriptures encourage us to keep our eyes focused not on our own misery, but on the blessings that follow. Colossians 3:1–4 says,

> If then you have been raised with Christ, seek the things that are above, where Christ is, seated at the right hand of God. Set your minds on things that are above, not on things that are on earth. For you have died, and your life is hidden with Christ in God. When Christ who is your life appears, then you also will appear with him in glory.

I'm struck by the phrase, "Christ who is your life." Christ is our life. Imagine that. To further personalize it, try saying aloud, "Christ is my life." If that's true, it should not be impossible to keep our eyes fixed on Him—*on heavenly things, not temporal ones.*

The purpose of suffering we're considering in this chapter is that God uses our sufferings to prepare us for eternal glory with Him. The Scriptures repeatedly juxtapose suffering and glory. Although these are opposing concepts, they are intricately interwoven. Romans 8:17 states, "Now if we are children, then we are heirs—heirs of God and co-heirs with Christ, if indeed we share in his sufferings in order that we may also share in his glory" (NIV). In fact, suffering and glory are so linked that sometimes it's difficult to see one without the other. Keeping that ultimate glory in sight will make it easier to overcome our suffering. In the verse with which I began this chapter, we're told that the reward for our perseverance through trials will be the Crown of Life. Therefore, the trials that come our way here serve to prepare us for heaven.

I once heard D. A. Carson say in a sermon preached at our church that our ultimate reward is the consummation of the relationship with God. It is a culmination of the work itself. Our life on earth is but a shadow of the one we will live eternally with our Savior. We must walk with Christ here, and we'll walk with Him better there. We must know God here, and we'll know Him better there. We must work for God here, and will work for God better there.

Along these same lines the apostle Paul wrote, "For I consider that the sufferings of this present time are not worth comparing with the glory that is to be revealed to us" (Rom. 8:18). Few of us have ever had to suffer to the degree Paul did, and yet he was able to make this remarkable statement. Our sufferings last for such a little while compared to the glories of heaven. Peter also reminded us of this when he wrote, "In this you rejoice, *though now for a little while,* if necessary, you have been grieved by various trials" (1 Peter 1:6, emphasis added).

We cannot afford to turn our attention away from Christ and instead focus on ourselves. When we do that, we exchange the spiritual for the worldly. There is already a tension that exists inside us between what we know we are to do in obedience to Christ and what our fleshly desires tempt us to do. That tension is spiritual warfare, pure and simple. Perhaps there is a battle raging within you right now. It may seem like the desires of the flesh are winning over the desires of the spirit. Our lifelong struggle is wanting what pleases us instead of what pleases God. When we focus on the many worldly things we desire, it causes us to take our eyes off the glories that await us in the future. For this reason, Paul explains in Philippians 3:13–14, "But one thing I do: forgetting what lies behind and straining forward to what lies ahead, I press on toward the goal for the prize of the upward call of God in Christ Jesus." Furthermore, Hebrews 12:1–2 tells us,

> Therefore, since we are surrounded by so great a cloud of witnesses, let us also lay aside every weight, and sin which clings so closely, and let us run with endurance the race that is set before us, looking to Jesus, the founder and perfecter of our faith, who for the joy that was set before him endured the cross, despising the shame, and is seated at the right hand of the throne of God.

Our worldly, fleshly desires may be symptoms of a larger issue, a heart issue. Sometimes, especially when we're hurting, we tend to look for comfort everywhere except the place that offers true comfort. When we seek this kind of quick relief from our suffering, our tendency is to latch onto the handiest solutions available. Pressing forward toward the prize takes effort and concentration, which are tough commodities to come by in the midst of tribulation. Yet, if we are to live spiritually mature lives, that is exactly what we must do. When we lift our eyes from our own pain, problems, desires, and emotions and fix them instead on Jesus Christ and the glories of heaven, we can then leave depression and painful loss behind and walk toward true contentment and joy.

Jesus Christ is our model and example, showing us that first there must be suffering before there can be glory. He was mocked, beaten, abused, arrested, tried, falsely accused, and crucified. He completed what He came to earth to do. He came here to do His Father's will, to live a sinless life, to suffer, to rise from the dead, and ascend to the glory from which He came. In doing this, He secured the salvation of all His children. First He had to suffer. Then He was glorified and will be glorified in a greater way when He comes again. Last time He came as the Suffering Servant. Next time He will come in majesty as the King of kings and Lord of lords.

Paul speaks of our Savior's glorious return in Titus 2:11–14:

> For the grace of God has appeared, bringing salvation for all people, training us to renounce ungodliness and worldly passions, and to live self-controlled, upright, and godly lives in the present age, waiting for *our blessed hope, the appearing of the glory of our great God and Savior Jesus Christ, who gave himself for us* to redeem us from all lawlessness and to purify for himself a people for his own possession who are zealous for good works. (emphasis added)

Christ also spoke of His return in glory in Mark 13:26. "And then they will see the Son of Man coming in clouds with great power and glory." If *Christ* first suffered and then was glorified, why are we surprised when *we* are called to suffer in preparation for upcoming glory? My pastor, Lance Quinn, once preached, "If you are headed for glory, you *will* suffer. There will be trials, tests, suffering, pain, and persecution in this life. Through the midst of that pain, because of that pain, as a learning tool for us, we will ultimately, through that pain reach glory."

When we suffer, we can be encouraged and comforted by the knowledge that through our suffering we are being prepared for ultimate glory with Christ. We do not rejoice in the suffering itself, but in the result of the suffering. "If you look at trials through God's perspective you can rejoice through your tears because you know God is building perseverance in your life and [you] cannot possibly be Christianly mature apart from such perseverance. And in the midst of your tears you can rejoice."[2]

Why don't we look at our trials through God's perspective? I believe it's because many times we are so focused on our own suffering that we don't look around the corner to the glory awaiting us. We become so locked into our own pain that we can't see anything else. Sometimes we may even say to ourselves, "I don't want any more spiritual maturity if this is what I must endure to attain it. I'm done. I'm as mature as I want to be." Pain and depression make us say things like that. However, though we have the responsibility to seek after spiritual wisdom, our level of understanding depends most of all on the Holy Spirit, who enables us to understand, to persevere, and ultimately to become spiritually mature. He determines the degree of sanctification we eventually attain.

Pastor Quinn made another good point in his sermon about suffering and glory. He said, "Do we say, 'I want the *suffering* but not the *glory?*' Of course not! But how many of us would say, 'I want the *glory* without the *suffering?*' That's different, isn't it? We *do* want the glory without the suffering!" I've heard Christians (sometimes jokingly and sometimes not) admonish others that they should never pray for patience. Why would they caution someone against that? It's because they have learned that patience is not just zapped into our character. Patience is brought about as a result of perseverance through trials of many kinds. So they warn others that praying for patience is like directly asking to be tried by the fire of adversity. However, if we are truly serious about developing the spiritual fruit of patience or perseverance, adversity should not be a thing to be avoided but a thing to be experienced, giving thanks for the ultimate blessing of spiritual maturity.

Don't get me wrong. I am not there yet. I don't pray that God will send me problems and trials. But I do pray that God will give me the grace to embrace the adversities He brings into my life with my eyes focused on the good they will produce in me and in those around me. I try to view the problems as a gift presented to me to make me better and stronger and bring me closer to Him. Time and again I have fallen far short of mastering this quality. But, by God's grace, I am moving closer toward the goal.

Jesus Christ is not some kind of divine spectator of human agony. He doesn't sit on His throne impotent and uncaring.

Both His love and His sovereignty are awesome and incomprehensible to our finite minds. So we are to trust Him to exercise His complete control over everything that happens in a careful, loving way. Our biblical response to evil, suffering, and loss is grounded in our personal relationship with Him. And through His strength and providence, we can overcome all adversity in a humble and submissive way. *First, we will have to experience the fiery trials of suffering, and we must do it with our eyes fixed on our ultimate destination—heaven and an eternity with our Savior.*

There is another sense in which our suffering results in ultimate glory and reward in the life to come. We're told, "To the one who conquers I will grant to eat of the tree of life, which is in the paradise of God. . . . The one who conquers will be clothed thus in white garments and I will never blot his name out of the book of life. . . . The one who conquers, I will grant him to sit with me on my throne, as I also conquered and sat down with my Father on his throne" (Rev. 2:7, 3:5, 3:21).

More than Conquerors through Him Who Loved Us

I've said that there are going to be significant rewards for us in heaven. In this section, let's discuss some specific rewards. Our rewards are indeed worth thinking about and anticipating, if we are heirs with Christ. We wouldn't have been told about them if that were not the case. Yet, I don't think they should be our primary motivation for obedience or our total focus in desiring heaven. If that were the case, we'd be looking toward heaven to fulfill ourselves for our own selfish gain. And that won't happen because greed does not exist in heaven.

However, it might serve to heighten our desire for heaven if we were to understand more about the rewards awaiting us there. "He who overcomes [those who have been saved by faith in Christ alone and persevere to the end] will *inherit all this, and I will be his God and he will be my son*" (Rev. 21:7 NIV, emphasis added). We will be more than servants in heaven, although if that were all we were it would still be much more than we deserve. Actually, we will be heirs of the kingdom, "heirs of God, and fellow heirs with Christ" (Rom. 8:17). John MacArthur writes:

> Heaven will be our home, and we will dwell there not as mere guests, but with all the privileges of family members—children of the master of the house. . . .
>
> Plainly, Scripture is teaching that all Christians will receive a full share of the inheritance of heaven. Every believer will 'inherit all things' (Rev. 21:7), so the inheritance isn't carved up and apportioned on the basis of worthiness. And when God says, 'I will be his God and he shall be my son'—He is saying that heaven will be not only our dwelling-place, but also our possession: We will be there not as boarders, but as full-fledged members of the family. What an inexpressible privilege that is.[3]

Here are a few more examples from Scripture of the rewards that await us in heaven:

> Henceforth there is laid up for me [Paul] *the crown of righteousness*, which the Lord, the righteous judge, will award to me on that Day, and not only to me but also to all who have loved his appearing. (2 Tim. 4:8, emphasis added)
>
> Blessed is the man who remains steadfast under trial, for when he has stood the test he will receive *the crown of life*, which God has promised to those who love him. (James 1:12, emphasis added)
>
> And when the chief Shepherd [Christ] appears, you will receive the unfading *crown of glory*. (1 Peter 5:4, emphasis added)
>
> Rejoice and be glad, *for your reward is great in heaven*. (Matt. 5:12, emphasis added)

I saved one of my favorite passages for last:

> Blessed be the God and Father of our Lord Jesus Christ! *According to his great mercy, he has caused us* to be born again to a living hope through the resurrection of Jesus Christ from the dead, *to an inheritance that is imperishable, undefiled, and unfading, kept in heaven for you,* who *by God's power* are *being guarded through faith* for a salvation ready to be revealed in the last time. In this you rejoice, though *now for a little while,* if necessary, you have been grieved by various trials, so that the tested genuineness of your faith—more precious than gold that perishes though it is tested by fire—may be found to result in praise and glory and honor at the revelation of Jesus Christ. Though you have not seen him, you love him. Though you do not now see him, you believe in him and rejoice with joy that is inexpressible and filled with glory, obtaining *the outcome of your faith, the salvation of your souls.* (1 Peter 1:3–9, emphasis added)

General Truths about Heaven

We've spoken of some of the specific rewards that await believers in heaven. Now let's briefly examine some of the general truths of heaven. An understanding of what we have to look forward to will make it that much easier to keep our eyes focused on the prize—eternal life in heaven with Christ.

- *Prepared for us by God*: Jesus told his disciples in John 14:1–3, "Let not your hearts be troubled. Believe in God; believe also in me. In my Father's house are many rooms. If it were not so, would I have told you that I go to prepare a place for you? And if I go and prepare a place for you, I will come again and will take you to myself, that where I am you may be also."
- *New bodies*: Here, our spirits are housed in flimsy, dirty, worn-out vessels that continuously break down and decay. In heaven, we will have new bodies that are imperishable! We don't know what they will look like,

but we know they will never be sick, never hurt, and never die.

- *Only joy*: No more sorrow, suffering, or crying.
- *Only holiness*: No sin of any kind will exist in heaven. That means that we will be perfectly Christlike at last.
- *Only reverence*: Our primary occupation in heaven will be the ceaseless worship of God as the object of our love and praise.
- *Only beauty*: Since heaven is designed by God without the contamination of sin, it is a place of unimaginable beauty. Now I believe God did a rather remarkable job on the creation of earth. I cannot imagine anything more beautiful than what He's already given us here. Yet the Bible tells us that, like so many other things, this creation is nothing but a shadow of what is to come! We don't know exactly what it will look like, but one thing is sure—heaven will be spectacular!

These are just a few of the rewards awaiting us in heaven. Suffice it to say that the sufferings we undergo here on earth, if we are believers in Christ, won't be all for nothing. They are not without purpose. They are not controlled by fate or chance or bad luck. No, they are part of God's divine orchestration and design of our lives. They are designed for our good not only while we're here on earth, but also for an eternity in heaven, where *eternal fellowship with Him will be our chief reward!*

○ ○ ○

Questions for Reflection

1. What does it mean to live our lives with the end in sight?
2. What are the two opposing concepts this chapter discusses? Which usually comes first? Do you ever find yourself desiring one and avoiding the other?

3. We're told to rejoice in our sufferings. Isn't that a bit masochistic? How is it possible to do this and what is the goal?
4. How can meditation on the glories of heaven serve to motivate you to persevere through suffering and trials?
5. According to this chapter, what will be our chief reward in heaven?

7

TO GIVE US OPPORTUNITIES TO WITNESS

> But even if you should suffer for righteousness' sake, you will be blessed. Have no fear of them, nor be troubled, but in your hearts regard Christ the Lord as holy, *always being prepared to make a defense to anyone who asks you for a reason for the hope that is in you.*
> —1 Peter 3:14–15 (emphasis added)

"For to Me to Live Is Christ"

Sometimes we speak louder by our actions than by our words. We have greater opportunities to reflect the love of Christ through adversity than through obvious blessing. A few years back, a friend of mine lay dying in a hospital bed when a sweet and caring nurse came to check on her. "Are you afraid?" she asked her, timidly. Matter-of-factly, my friend said, "Of course not! I'm a Christian!" I still smile when I remember that. When people witness our godly response to adversity and suffering, they may ask us the source of such an attitude. We should be

8

prepared to give the reasons for this uncommon outlook on suffering (uncommon to the world without Christ) and for the hope He has given us.

The courage and devotion of the men and women of the Bible demonstrate that truth. Even now, their attitudes and responses to hardship and suffering serve to teach us, to encourage us, and even to inspire us to adopt those same qualities. I once had the blessing of being seated next to Dr. Joseph Tson at an event held in his honor at our church. Dr. Tson is a well-known and beloved man of God who faithfully ministers in Romania. He has dealt with persecution and threats to his life on many occasions. His home has been invaded and his library destroyed. He has been followed, questioned, and jailed. The Communist party dealt him many blows, but he faced them with courage and spoke to them of the blessedness of Christ.

He told us about one of the times when his life was threatened. He stood up to the Communist soldier holding him at gunpoint and said, "Go ahead and kill me. For the moment you do, my words will take flight and spread to all the world! My tapes and my books will flourish! You will make my words more powerful by killing me than they could ever be if you don't." As a result, not only was he spared, but a proclamation was issued that under no circumstances was he to be harmed. Suddenly the Communist party was looking out for him, actually protecting his safety! They knew the words he spoke were true and they didn't want to martyr him.

The way Dr. Tson handled such adversity in his life inspired me to want to respond in the same way, should I ever be in such a position. But if he had not been under such trial, I probably would never have heard of him, and his life would not have been such an example to me, and to thousands of others. His adversity increased his effectiveness as a witness for Christ. The same principle applies to you and me. We have the opportunity through the way we handle suffering, pain, and death to speak loudly and clearly to those around us. They can sense our devastation and despair or they can see the quiet, accepting submission to God's will in our lives, whatever that entails.

Remember the man in Luke 8? He was possessed by a legion of demons and Christ mercifully cast them out of him. This was a man who had run around naked for a long time, running across the countryside, and living among the tombs. Though the people had chained him, his superhuman strength allowed him to rip the chains and shackles apart. Jesus cast the demons out from him and immediately the man was restored to his right mind. His response? "The man from whom the demons had gone begged that he might be with him" (Luke 8:38). Jesus denied him that privilege but gave the command, " 'Return to your home, and declare how much God has done for you' " (Luke 8:39). Imagine what a powerful witness that man was for Christ.

Charles Spurgeon wrote,

> If Jesus loves you, and you are sick, let all the world see how you glorify God in your sickness. Let friends and nurses see how the beloved of the Lord are cheered and comforted by him. Let your holy resignation astonish them, and set them ad-miring your Beloved, who is so gracious to you that he makes you happy in pain, and joyful at the gates of the grave. If your religion is worth anything it ought to support you now, and it will compel unbelievers to see that he whom the Lord loveth is in better case when he is sick than the ungodly when full of health and vigour.[1]

My son and daughter-in-law inspired me by the way they over-came their sorrow and disappointment when the negligence of an obstetrician cost them the ability to conceive a child. Though both yearned to be parents, they have been denied that privilege. My daughter-in-law, Carrie, was especially devastated by this situ-ation, suffering physical and emotional agony because of it. But at the end of her journey, she was able to call the physician and tell him, "As long as I hold onto anger and hatred, I am hurting myself. I have to move on and in order to do that, I want you to know that I have forgiven you. I will not hold this against you any longer." I respect her for doing this because I know how hard it must have been. She came to realize that their situation did not exist outside of God's will. Still saddened by their inability to conceive, they have nonetheless come out of their initial devastation and found peace and forgiveness at its end. Now they have a great chance to witness to others who have to deal with similar heartbreak and disappointment. Because of their suffering, they have become stronger witnesses of the goodness of God in their lives.

The apostle Paul wrote, "For to me to live is Christ, and to die is gain. If I am to live in the flesh, that means fruitful labor for me. Yet which I shall choose I cannot tell. I am hard pressed between the two. *My desire is to depart and be with Christ, for that is far better.* But *to remain in the flesh is more necessary on your account*" (Phil. 1:21–24, emphasis added). Do you think this is an unrealistic attitude? Although Paul is exemplary, the attitude he demonstrates here is attainable by the grace of God. The more we grow in the understanding of who He is and in our relationship with Christ, the more we can embrace these same thoughts.

John Piper writes, "God is most magnified in us when we are most satisfied in him."[2] That satisfaction comes from learning all we can about Him. We should revel in His sufficiency, stand in awe of His power and majesty, and yet be humbled by His love, grace, and mercy. Along with the words of the Bible, suffering and adversity teach us God's utter reliability and faithfulness to His promises. We learn to trust Him with our lives, which includes our infirmities, heartache, and even death. When we are that trusting, we can't help but reflect His light to the world around us!

○ ○ ○

Questions for Reflection

1. How can we serve as a witness for Christ through the way we handle adversity?

81

2. If someone asked you how you remain so hopeful and cheerful in the midst of trial, what would you tell them?

3. Is there room for histrionics in the lives of believers? What might onlookers assume about the person who claims to be a Christian yet falls apart at the seams when things get tough?

4. My son and daughter-in-law could have ended up bitter and angry about what happened to them. How does their godly attitude serve to honor Christ?

5. How have you handled tough situations in the past? Will the thoughts expressed in this chapter help you react differently the next time you're faced with trouble? Why? Or why not?

TO MAKE US MORE GRATEFUL AND APPRECIATIVE

Because *your steadfast love is better than life*, my lips will praise you. So I will bless you as long as I live; in your name I will lift up my hands. My soul will be satisfied as with fat and rich food, and *my mouth will praise you with joyful lips*, when I remember you upon my bed, and meditate on you in the watches of the night; *for you have been my help, and in the shadow of your wings I will sing for joy*.

—Psalm 63:3–7 (emphasis added)

Deliverance Leads to Gratitude and Joy

There would be no need for God to intervene in our trials if our lives were free from suffering. That would be more like, well, heaven! That's what we have to look forward to. But as long as we live on this earth, we will have troubles.

When we have been rescued from the fire of adversity our hearts overflow with joy and gratitude. I'm reminded of stories

I've heard of people who have been rescued from danger and adversity. What do you hear from their lips? Complaints? "Why did this happen to me?" No, you hear them saying, "Thank you," to all those involved in their rescue. You hear things like, "I will never be able to express my gratitude for . . ." That happens to us too when we are hard pressed by life's circumstances. Yes, going through trial and tribulation is tough, but when the suffering has passed, we are filled to overflowing with gratitude to the Lord. I opened this chapter with one of my favorite psalms. Notice what it says: "for you have been my help." Sometimes He brings us suffering in order to cause us to remember our own helplessness and His utter sufficiency. When we reflect on what God has done for us, our natural response is gratitude.

Have you ever noticed that during the good times, we have a tendency to think of God less? Have you ever noticed how subtly our minds turn from absolute dependence on Him to an attitude of self-sufficiency when everything seems to go our way? We begin to believe we're actually in control of our lives. We're sinful creatures who tend to forget just who is in charge. But when we're faced with something definitely out of our control, we remember and turn to Him with utter dependence and gratitude.

Mary's Gratitude

When I think about biblical thankfulness and gratitude, I sometimes reflect on Mary Magdalene, Christ's faithful follower. We're not told a lot about Mary's past except that her name was Mary, she was from Magdala, and Christ cast out seven demons from her. That's it. We don't know if she was young or old, beautiful or plain, fat or thin, or rich or poor. (By the way, the Scriptures never say she was a prostitute, which is something I've heard time and again from the media, movies, books, and even pastors!)

Though we're not told much about her before she met the Lord, we are told a lot about demon possession. In every case, there were similarities. For instance, we know that none of the demon possessed ever came to Christ for healing. They were either brought to Him or He met them along the way. We know they were utterly tormented by the demons inside them and were, therefore, not in any condition to lead normal lives. They were outcasts from society who lived utterly ruined lives. Some were so miserable they would cut or bruise themselves with stones. Some ran around naked and wailing. We know that demoniacs weren't referred to as sinners, but as victims. The main thing we know is that there was nothing in this natural world that could relieve them from their perpetual agony. They lived in a state of utter hopelessness. So, though we're not told the specifics of Mary's possession, we are told there were *seven* demons in her. From that, we can safely assume she was in a desperate condition of endless torment with no hope of ever having a normal life.

Then came Jesus. We're told nothing more than that He cast out seven demons. We're not told how He did it. We're just told that He did it. Put yourself in Mary Magdalene's shoes for a moment. Imagine her agony. And then, suddenly and instantaneously (because that's how He rescued the demoniacs mentioned in the New Testament), Jesus cast these demons from her and left her in a state of peace. Can you imagine the inexpressible joy and gratitude she must have felt for her Savior? He not only brought her new spiritual life but also gave her physical life back to her. No wonder she was one of His most devoted followers.

The Gerasene demoniac's response to Jesus was the same. In Luke 8:35–39, we read,

Then people went out to see what had happened, and they came to Jesus and found the man from whom the demons had gone, *sitting at the feet of Jesus, clothed and in his right mind*, and they were afraid. . . The man from whom the demons had gone *begged that he might be with him*, but Jesus sent him away, saying, "Return to your home, and declare how much God has done for you." And he went away, proclaiming throughout the whole city how much Jesus had done for him.

His response for the relief Jesus Christ had given him was that he wanted to accompany Jesus and stay by His side. Jesus didn't grant that request but gave him another mission—to spread the word of what He had done for him.

In the same way, it's not unreasonable that Mary Magdalene would want to devote the rest of her life to ministering to this man who gave her life and rescued her from a life of hopeless darkness. Wouldn't you do that if He had done the same for you? Well, guess what. He did! Every one of us who claims Christ as Lord was rescued from darkness, from eternal separation from Him, and brought into His glorious light, love, and righteousness. All of us owe Him the same kind of love and undying gratitude Mary Magdalene so sweetly modeled for us.

Christianity is different from any other religion. All the others have some kind of ladder by which one can climb to supposedly reach "god." But in the case of Christianity, although there is also a ladder, we don't have to climb it to reach God, because He came down the ladder to rescue us. Our salvation is accomplished through His work, not our own. For this, we should be eternally grateful. Peter said, "But you are a chosen race, a royal priesthood, a holy nation, a people for his own possession, *that you may proclaim the excellencies of him who called you out of darkness into his marvelous light*" (1 Peter 2:9, emphasis added). The motivation for this proclamation to the world is not out of a grudging sense of duty and obligation. The motivation springs from a heart bursting with gratitude to our Savior and our help in time of need.

Some of us may have been taught that the way we glorify God is through duty, not delight. Actually, our delight in Him *is* our duty!

Delight yourself in the LORD,
　　and he will give you the desires of your heart.
Commit your way to the LORD;
　　trust in him, and he will act. (Ps. 37:4–5)

Note that there is a cause and effect in this passage. We are to delight ourselves in the Lord, commit our way to Him and trust in Him. That's the first part of the equation. The consequence is that He will give us the desires of our hearts. In fact, when we do those things consistently as a part of our daily walk with Christ the desires of our heart transform little by little into *His* desires. When we genuinely value the fulfillment of His will, our desires will fall right in line with His.

Our Sufferings Cause Us to See More Clearly

You've heard the stories again and again. Someone is diagnosed with a terminal disease and suddenly they gain a new appreciation for the world around them. Even the little things seem so precious. Their priorities change with their new perspective and they see life like they've never seen it before. They learn to stop and smell the roses and to look around at all the beauty in this world.

I've seen this scenario so many times. Even the air we breathe seems fresher. Colors are more vibrant. The world is more beautiful. The touch of a hand is dearer, sweeter somehow. We stop taking for granted those things and those people we've scarcely noticed in the past. One of my on-going campaigns with my children, my husband, my parents, and my friends has been to encourage them to take note of those precious things. Stop and smell the roses now! Don't wait until something tragic occurs before you decide to stop your busyness long enough to notice the beauty and the wonder and the sweetness of the world around you.

I learned not to take things for granted a long time ago. When I was young I overheard someone crying at a funeral, "Oh, if only he knew how much he meant to me. There are so many things I wish I had told him." I decided then and there that I would never have the need to say that. The people I love would know how much they mean to me all the time, not just on their deathbed. That's one reason I encourage the family members I work with to talk to their loved one who is dying. I encourage them to talk about the things they want them to know while they can still understand and respond to them. *I am giving you the same advice. Tell them you love them and tell them goodbye before it's too late to do so. You may not have another chance and I don't want you to live with regret.* My grandmother used to say, "Don't send me flowers after I'm gone. Send them to me now so I can enjoy them!" And I did!

When we live lives of gratitude to the Lord, we have fewer regrets. As more grateful people, we acknowledge our dependence on Him who may take us through some hard places, but who is always there to guide, guard, and bring us safely through our trials. "*I will turn their mourning into joy*; I will comfort them, and *give them gladness for sorrow*" (Jer. 31:13, emphasis added).

If there were no suffering, how would we even recognize the good times? If we didn't feel bad every now and then, why would we ever thank God for the times when we are pain free and feeling great? Wouldn't we just assume that was the way things were and take those times for granted? Suffering occurs in our lives to give us the contrast we need to become grateful for what we have. A person familiar with suffering doesn't take the little things for granted. Neither should we.

Questions for Reflection

1. Psalm 63 says that God's love is better than life. Is that something you believe to be true in your own life?

2. What is our response when we reflect on what God has done for us?
3. Why do we tend to think more about God when we're going through something hard, as opposed to those periods when we seem to float through life without a worry?
4. What similarities do we share with those who have been rescued from demon possession? In the case of their demon possession and our own condition of spiritual darkness, what or who was our only hope?
5. Our obedience to and affection for Christ should not be motivated by a grudging sense of duty and obligation. What should motivate our obedience instead?

TO EQUIP US
TO COMFORT OTHERS

Blessed be the God and Father of our Lord Jesus Christ, the Father of mercies and *God of all comfort, who comforts us in all our affliction, so that we may be able to comfort those who are in any affliction, with the comfort with which we ourselves are comforted by God.* For as we share abundantly in Christ's sufferings, so through Christ we share abundantly in comfort too.

—2 Corinthians 1:3–5 (emphasis added)

The Gift That Keeps on Giving

So far in our examination of the purposes of suffering and death, we've discovered some of the personal benefits they bring to us and the glory they bring to God. But we haven't discussed how they prepare us to benefit others, which is a vital function. *Suffering is meant to be spiritually productive.* God's blessings to us are generous and gracious. They are so much more than we deserve. However, blessings are not to be held onto but are designed to extend outward to those with whom we come into contact. In fact, wanting to share what we've been given is an appropriate response to such blessings.

Previously, I've referred to the comfort God gives us. He is, after all, the God of all comfort. However, in this chapter we will discuss comfort from a different perspective. When I think of comfort from God, I think about a vertical transaction. Comfort comes from above. However, the kind of comfort I visualize in this chapter is a horizontal transaction. It takes place between people. We not only give comfort to others, but also receive it from them!

One of the reasons we go through trials and tribulations is to equip us to comfort others. Billy Graham wrote that his mom used to say, "God doesn't comfort us to make us *comfortable*, but to make us *comforters*."[1] Repeatedly, God leads us outside our comfort zones for positive and beneficial reasons. If He did not bring us pain, we would never experience comfort or relief. We wouldn't learn how to extend it to others. We are to *use* our pain. Instead of basking in the acceptance of comfort from others, we should look for opportunities to serve, to distribute to others the kind of comfort we've been given.

For those who have a self-centered approach to life, this concept makes absolutely no sense at all. They want to dwell on their own pain and to wallow in their self-pity. They find it difficult to move outside the boundary of their suffering in order to see those around them whose needs may be even greater than their own. But to the servant whose purpose in life is to glorify God, it makes perfect sense. God softens our hearts. He gives us the command to "bear one another's burdens, and so fulfill the law of Christ" (Gal. 6:2). We are to "rejoice with those who rejoice, weep with those who weep" (Rom. 12:15). We glorify God when we seek to comfort others.

In Matthew 25:34–40, one of my favorite passages, Jesus tells His disciples,

Then the King will say to those on his right, "Come, you who are blessed by my Father, inherit the kingdom prepared for you from the foundation of the world. For I was hungry and you gave me food, I was thirsty and you gave me drink, I was a stranger and you welcomed me, I was naked and you clothed me, I was sick and you visited me, I was in prison and you came to me." Then the righteous will answer him, saying, "Lord, when did we see you hungry and feed you, or thirsty and give you drink? And when did we see you a stranger and welcome you, or naked and clothe you? And when did we see you sick or in prison and visit you?" And the King will answer them, "Truly, I say to you, as you did it to one of the least of these my brothers, you did it to me."

Sometimes this passage motivates greater service to others. When I perform some act of kindness, I might think to myself, "This is just as if I were doing it for the Lord." When I think of my service to others with this in mind, it's amazing how it energizes my desire to serve. Not only does it perk up my heart and attitude, but it also nudges my brain into thinking of more and better ways to serve. This passage can be an important tool when service or comfort to another is necessary but your heart isn't in it. When we're honest with ourselves, we must confess this to be the case on occasion. But to think of serving or comforting Christ should rid our hearts of any resistance. Call upon this tool whenever you need such an attitude adjustment! It does amazing things when your tenderness levels are low. Serve others as you would serve your Lord. Because whenever we show the slightest kindness to others He counts it as service to Himself. What a gracious Lord we serve!

I've heard it said, "Don't waste the pain! Use it for good!" God does not bless us and intend for the blessing to stop with us. That blessing has the capacity to keep going and going and going. Because He has blessed us with His comfort, we can pass that blessing on to others who can in turn pass it on to others. What a beautiful concept—the continuity of comfort.

What Does It Mean to Comfort Others?

Some people just seem like natural comforters, don't they? Let's face it; some people are better at this than others. Having a knack for empathetic service is a gift from God. But that doesn't mean that we can't all become comforters. We're not off the hook because it doesn't come naturally to us.

It's a little like the gift of evangelism. Some people are just better at it than others. God gives the gift to some, and yet we are all called to spread the good news about Jesus Christ. We're told in Matthew 28:19–20, "Go, therefore and make disciples of all nations, baptizing them in the name of the Father and of the Son and of the Holy Spirit, teaching them to observe all that I have commanded you." Christ tells His disciples (which includes us, if we are also followers of Christ) that as we go about our lives, we are to spread the word, make disciples (evangelism), and then baptize them and teach them how to live a life of obedience to Him (discipleship). He didn't say, "Those of you who feel you have a natural gift for this should do it and the rest of you are off the hook."

In the same way, 2 Timothy 4:2 urges us to "preach the Word; be prepared in season and out of season; correct, rebuke and encourage—with great patience and careful instruction" (NIV). Whether you have the "gift of evangelism" or not, you are to "honor Christ the Lord as holy, always being prepared to make a defense to anyone who asks you for a reason for the hope that is in you" (1 Peter 3:15). Folks, we're clearly not off the hook in the area of evangelism, and the same goes for comforting others. As we've already seen, God comforts us "so that we may be able to comfort those who are in any affliction" (2 Cor. 1:4). That means all of us, not just those who feel really comfortable with it. Therefore, many of us will need a few ideas about how to minister to the hurting. Don't worry if it doesn't come easily to you. God will bless you as you learn!

Sometimes people tell me they don't know what to say to comfort others. I tell them not to worry about it. Sometimes you don't have to say a word to be a comforter. Sometimes all the words in the world don't have the impact that one long, silent hug can have on a newly grieving person. A hug that says, "I'm trying to understand how you feel, and I'm so sorry, and I do so want to help!" Many times, a person may not remember what you *told* them during that sad time. But they'll remember the comfort you were able to offer them. Your very presence will speak volumes.

At times the most comforting thing you can say is the truth about how you're feeling: "I want so badly to be able to say or do something that would be a comfort to you right now. But I don't know what to do or the right words to say. But please know that I do care." You see? Totally honest. Totally sincere. And you know what? It would be totally appreciated. Comforting others doesn't need to be difficult. It's about expressing concern for others. You don't have to know all the answers. You just have to care about people.

I'm reminded of a little story someone sent me over the Internet. I don't know the author's name, but the story demonstrates my point. "Author and lecturer Leo Buscaglia once talked about a contest he was asked to judge. The purpose of the contest was to find the most caring child. The winner was a four-year-old child whose next-door neighbor was an elderly gentleman who had recently lost his wife. Upon seeing the man cry, the little boy went into the old gentleman's yard, climbed onto his lap, and just sat there. When his mother asked him what he had said to the neighbor, the little boy said, 'Nothing, I just helped him cry.' "

Many have expressed frustration because they wanted to pray with a sorrowing friend or relative, or to talk to them from the Scriptures, but they didn't know how to get started. What I do is ask permission. It not only provides a way to get started, but it prevents you from doing something that may not be comforting to the person at that specific time. Say something simple like, "I'd like to say a prayer for you. Would you mind?" or "Would you mind if I pray for you?" Most people will nod or say yes to a request like that. Then you can take that person's hand, or put a loving hand on his shoulder, if you feel comfortable doing so. A touch speaks louder than words and creates instant intimacy. There is such power in touch. Then just say a simple and sincere prayer.

I advise keeping prayers short and sweet. When grieving or hurting, a person's attention span is short. In most cases, they don't want a New Testament survey or long, flowery, preachy prayers. Make your prayer relevant to them. If you'd like to express some spiritual truth you believe relevant and comforting to someone's specific need, you might start with, "I'm reminded of a passage of scripture I've always found comforting and helpful in times like these. Would you mind if I read some of it to you?" Again, few will decline if the request is made from a caring, loving heart.

But be careful. There are also words that can hurt. In our effort to comfort, at times we can come off sounding superior or insincere. Sometimes we offer platitudes, like, "Well, this is the Lord's will," or "There's going to be good that will come from this." True enough, but in your friend's situation, it may not be the time to say such things.

When a person's heart is freshly broken, you may want to express your love with caring hugs and softly spoken words of understanding. God may give you the opportunity to encourage someone with these words at a later date, but not in the midst of current suffering. And please don't express messages with an "I told you so" in there. It's just not the proper time for that. "Hurting people require an enormous energy just to survive. We can be a further drain on their energies through insensitive remarks or neglect, or we can provide an atmosphere of love that makes it easier for them to experience God's comfort."[2]

Let's Get Specific

Sometimes when people are hurting they just can't talk. At these times you might offer to talk to them when they're ready.

Let them know that you will be a good listener when the time comes even though you don't have all the answers. Many people will tell the grieving person, "Call me if you want to talk" or "Call me if you need anything." But few will actually follow up, and in most cases the person will not take you up on your offer. That's why it's important to follow up with them in a few days, again in a few weeks, and again in a few months. Instead of saying, "Do you need anything?" phrase your question in a more effective way. A closed-ended question can too easily be answered in the negative. Instead ask, "What can I do for you?" or "How may I pray for you?" or "How can I help?" Questions like this usually receive a positive answer. Being specific is also an important part of helping someone who is suffering. I've listed below sample questions and statements to help you be more specific:

- "I'm going to the grocery store later. May I pick up some items for you?" They will be more likely to allow you to help them if you ask to do something specific.
- If you want to help a friend who is the primary care-giver for an ailing loved one, you might say, "I am planning to come over in a little while. Why don't you let me sit with your husband for a couple of hours while you take a nap, a long bath, or just get out of the house for a bit?" Caregivers are so used to taking lightning-quick showers that a long soak in the tub becomes a tremendous luxury. Likewise, being able to go out to lunch with a friend, run to the grocery store, or take a nap when you don't have to worry about taking care of someone can be extremely refreshing.
- "I'm on my way over to your place to help with the housework. I know you must be exhausted and it's just a way I'd like to pitch in. Shall I bring us something to eat for lunch first?"
- "I picked up some lovely flowers for you this morning. Mind if I drop them off in an hour or two?" When

you get there to drop off the flowers, step inside the door when it's opened. You might say something like, "I have a few minutes before I have to get home. Mind if I stay for a cup of coffee?" Use discernment here. There are times when a person just needs to be alone. You don't want to be a drain on what little energy they have left.

- "I offered to be there for you if you need someone to talk to. I was really serious about that. I have some time today. Why don't we go for a drive in the country and just talk?"

- When a person is grieving, little things like mowing the lawn, sweeping the porch, or weeding the garden get ignored. Instead of *saying anything* you might just go over and do these things without being asked. Be creative in serving each other. Look for a need and fill it.

- Often the person is absolutely sick and tired of company and they just want to be left alone to take a nap, think, or cry. A sweet offer at this time might be to say "Why don't I come over and entertain your guests while you lie down for a bit? I can answer the phone for you and run interference with any unannounced visitors."

- A week or so after the painful event, it often helps to do something physical to reduce stress and grief-related fatigue. To help get them moving, try saying, "It's such a beautiful day today. When was the last time you got out of the house and went for a nice walk? Why don't I pick you up and we can go to the park for a walk? You don't have to talk if you don't want to, but a walk in the fresh air might do us both some good. Would 1:30 or 2:00 be better for you?"

These are merely some examples of ways to comfort a grieving person. But there are no limits to the number of ways we can help. Regardless of which method we use to comfort others—whether through words, acts, or cards—we are told to do so. *We are not to hold on to our blessings of comfort. We are to freely give to others what we have received from God. That continuity of comfort makes a big difference to a hurting world.*

Questions for Reflection

1. How many times was the word "comfort" used in 2 Corinthians 1:3–5? What does this tell you?
2. How is this purpose of suffering different from the others we've discussed so far?
3. What is the "continuity of comfort" described in this chapter? See if you can articulate this concept to someone else.
4. According to Mrs. Graham, "God doesn't comfort us to make us _____, but to make us _____." Memorize this beautifully simple statement.
5. The concept of comforting others won't make much sense to someone who is wrapped up in their own misery. Why not?

Purposes Specific to Some Suffering

TO TEACH US GOD'S LAW

It is good for me that I was afflicted, that I might learn your statutes. The law of your mouth is better to me than thousands of gold and silver pieces.

—Psalm 119:71–72

God's Word Is Precious

The psalmist above shows a correct response to affliction. He certainly had a love for God's Word, for His commands, His decrees, and His laws. He saw them as being more valuable than worldly wealth—than thousands of gold and silver pieces. How valuable is God's Word to you? As much as I love the Word of God, I confess I fall desperately short of the kind of passion for God's law described in Psalm 119. I encourage you to read the whole psalm to get a true picture of how important God's statutes are to the psalmist. The writer yearned for God's Word. He serves as an excellent example and standard for the rest of us, and in this psalm, he teaches us that affliction drives us to the Word. "Before I was afflicted I went astray, but now I keep your word" (Ps. 119:67).

We have a tendency to take the Word of God for granted. We assume we will always have it. Yet there have been times in history when the possession of the Bible resulted in death or imprisonment. There are no guarantees that we will always have His Word readily available to us. There may be a time when possession of a Bible or attendance of any kind of corporate worship of Jesus Christ may be prohibited. Therefore we should avail ourselves of the priceless truths it teaches.

The Word of God is precious. It is the source of our knowledge of the Father, the Son, and the Holy Spirit. Let us not waste time while our Bibles gather dust on a forgotten bookshelf. Let us learn, study, and meditate upon its truths. Let us commit as much of it to our memories as possible and store it in our hearts. When we stumble and fall, or when adversity overtakes us, we will look to His promises again and again. Meditation on His attributes is like a salve to our broken hearts.

The Word of God was so precious to Paul that he urged Timothy to bring it to him while in prison in Rome. 2 Timothy 4:13 says, "When you come, bring the cloak that I left with Carpus at Troas, also the books, and above all the parchments." Obviously the cloak was for physical comfort, but the parchments were for his spiritual needs. He wrote, "above all" to signify that the parchments were the most important things he needed and wanted. That's how precious they were to him. Let us treasure the Scriptures like Paul and as the psalmist did:

> I have stored up your word in my heart,
>   that I might not sin against you.
> Blessed are you, O LORD;
>   teach me your statutes!
>
>   . . . .
>
> I will meditate on your precepts
>   and fix my eyes on your ways.
> I will delight in your statutes;
>   I will not forget your word. (Ps. 119:11–12, 15–16)

Suffering Sends Us to God's Word

Adversity drives us to our Bibles and therefore to our Father. Our trials and sorrows serve to teach us the decrees of God and to bring them home to us more fully. Our circumstances can bring us to a place where we hungrily turn to the Word of God in order to seek answers to the questions brought about by sorrow. I urge you to be diligent in your study of the Scriptures.

However, there are times when we may need a little help with our problems. Sometimes we find ourselves embroiled in a problem that we can't figure out. We might even turn to the Bible and still not see God's clear instruction for our present difficulty. In these times of confusion, please consider making an appointment to talk with a biblical counselor. Many people think that biblical counseling involves listening to someone who is aloof, brainy, and definitely holier-than-thou spout appropriate scriptures at us. Although this description may accurately depict some counselors, this in no way characterizes biblical counseling.

When you receive biblical counseling, you will find people with sympathetic hearts who long to lovingly come alongside you. They will listen to your story, obtain a complete history, and then prayerfully seek to apply God's word to your situation while guiding you to the Scriptures, godly obedience, and our merciful Lord. They will also try to alleviate the pain that caused you to seek help in the first place. I have studied biblical counseling from one of the pioneers in the field, Dr. Wayne Mack. Initially, the reason I began my course of study was to increase my effectiveness in counseling others. But as I learned from this compassionate and wise man, I noticed how he repeatedly directed me back to the Scriptures in a way that strengthened my walk with the Lord. Hopefully this experience has equipped me to be a better, wiser counselor to those who need support.

Our painful circumstances may be the tool God uses to guide us to a gentle counselor who will facilitate our growth in spiritual maturity and in grace. I say "facilitate" because the growth and maturity comes not from the wise counselor but from the Holy Spirit, our great Counselor. Even if our troubles land us in biblical counseling, it is clear that adversity often results in driving us back to the Bible. Since God teaches us through adversity, it is our responsibility to learn from it.

How Do We Do That?

1) *We must submit to God's will.* Our submission should not be a reluctant or sullen one—not as the defeated general submits to his conqueror, but voluntarily. If we complain about the situations in which He places us, we are actually grumbling against Him and our insolence flies in the face of God. We dare not do this! Instead, our submission should be sweet and humble, like a darling child who falls into our outstretched arms. We submit to His will in the same way a patient on the operating table submits to the skilled hands of the surgeon—with complete trust.

We should ask God to give us submission to His will even when we don't understand it. What's harder is this kind of submission when His will clearly goes against our own desires. More and more my prayers sound something like this, "Conform my will to Yours, Lord. I want to glory in Your design for my life. Give me the grace to humbly submit to *whatever* Your will is for this situation. Enable me to want what You want." When we pray in this way, we can rest assured that God will always grant us the desires of our hearts because the desires of our hearts will line up with His perfect will. His purposes are *always* accomplished.

2) *We must bring the Word of God to bear on the situation.* We must pray that God will reveal passages to us in the Scriptures

that will illumine our situations and circumstances. The Holy Spirit applies these passages to our hearts and only through this do we receive the grace to trust God through any adversity. *The Scriptures help us to better understand adversity, and in turn, adversity helps us to better understand the Scriptures.* "For the LORD gives wisdom; from his mouth come knowledge and understanding" (Prov. 2:6). We are to look to Him for wisdom. One thing is certain—He will not zap wisdom into your head. You must sincerely ask Him for it in prayer. You must devote significant time and effort into the reading and study of His Word, and you must meditate upon this Word to glean its application to your life.

The Scriptures have an unusual quality. I can read and even study a passage and take away from that study an understanding of what the passage teaches. As the situations in my life change and my experiences grow, I can read the same passage and, bam, it's as though I'd never read it before! I suddenly find some truth I'd missed in every previous reading. Frequently I find myself saying, "How could I have missed that?"

Knowledge of the Scriptures deepens with repetition. I think of it sometimes as being a little like baklava, my favorite Greek pastry. Its truths exist in layers of delicious sweetness! The first time through a passage you understand the first layer of meaning. In subsequent meditations on the same passage you discover another layer, and then another. In that way, no one can say they know everything there is to know about the Bible. If you hear someone make such a claim, don't believe them.

3) *We must remember our adversities in order to profit from the lessons they teach us.* God won't remove adversity until we have received the benefit it was intended to produce. That's what wisdom is all about. You take the lessons you've learned from the experiences God has given you and apply that knowledge to similar situations in the future. Adversity makes us wiser only if we can make that application.

One way to look at this is to think of a doorway with a very low opening. The first time you walk under it you might bump your head. The next time you'd remember the bump and duck down to avoid another one. People who cannot apply lessons learned simply keep bumping their heads every time they go through the door! I hope none of us is like that. Let's pray that God gives us the grace to apply the lessons He's teaching us.

Questions for Reflection

1. According to this chapter, what important purpose might our suffering serve? Would you be as likely to turn to God's Word if you weren't experiencing these problems?
2. What suggestions were made to facilitate learning from our adversities?
3. What's the difference between surrendering to a conquering army and submitting to a surgical procedure? How would you describe the way you submit to God's authority?
4. What happens to our will when we increasingly spend time in the study of God's Word? Look up John 3:29–31. What similarities do you see in John the Baptist's attitude of submission with the submission described in this chapter?
5. At the end of this chapter I said, "Adversity makes you wiser only if we can make that application." What application was I talking about?

TO DEMONSTRATE GOD'S LOVE

My son, do not despise the LORD's discipline or be weary
of his reproof, *for the LORD reproves him whom he loves*, as
a father the son in whom he delights.
                    —Proverbs 3:11–12 (emphasis added)

"If You Really Loved Me . . ."

Suffering and death occur to demonstrate God's love? It certainly doesn't seem like it, does it? Instead, it sometimes seems
like God has something against you, doesn't it? But that's not
the case at all.

As a parent, maybe you've run into the following situation
as you've tried to practice godly discipline with your children.
One of your children did something she was clearly told not
to do. Perhaps your means of discipline is to tell the child that
she may not go to the sleepover Friday evening with the rest
of her girlfriends. She looks at you with that mixture of anger
and hurt and blurts, "If you really loved me, you'd let me go."
What a great opportunity to share the above verse with her. You
tell her, "It's because I *do* love you that I must discipline you,

in obedience to God's Word. If I didn't love you, it wouldn't matter *what* you did. I simply wouldn't care!"

We discipline our children because we *do* love them. The same is true of our Father in heaven. He says in Hebrews 12:7–8, "It is for discipline that you have to endure. God is treating you as sons. For what son is there whom his father does not discipline? If you are left without discipline, in which all have participated, then you are illegitimate children and not sons." Our earthly fathers may exercise that discipline fairly and with discernment, but even the best father is still an imperfect being. Imperfection is not something we need to worry about with our heavenly Father. He exercises this discipline perfectly because He is perfect. He will never discipline us because of unrighteous anger. His discipline won't ever be harsher than it should be, and sometimes His grace and mercy means we don't get the severity we actually deserve! He is a gracious, loving Father.

We do not have a God who is subject to the moods that sway our own attitudes and behaviors. He never gets up on the wrong side of the bed. In James 1:17 we read, "Every good and perfect gift is from above, coming down from the Father of the heavenly lights, *who does not change like shifting shadows*" (NIV, emphasis added). In one of his sermons D. A. Carson said, "God does not have bad days. He doesn't get up one morning and say, 'Boy, do I feel grumpy today!' He is *invariably* good and can be nothing *but* good."[1] God doesn't cause or allow events into our lives just because of some sudden irrational whim, or because He's got it in for us that day. "God does not exercise His sovereignty capriciously, but only in such a way as His infinite love deems best for us."[2] He is faithful to keep His promises and one of those promises is that He will work everything for our *good* (see Romans 8:28). And as we're reminded in Romans 8:29, He does this for the purpose of conforming us to the image of His Son: "For those whom he foreknew he also predestined to be conformed to the image of his Son, in order that he might be the firstborn among many brothers." So, even the affliction we encounter is a demonstration of His kindness toward us.

The *result* will be for our good. The affliction is the tool He uses to accomplish the result.

Anytime God Brings Good from Suffering, It Is a Demonstration of His Love for Us

Regardless of which purpose God intends for our suffering, if He brings good out of it, it is a demonstration of His love for us. For instance, sometimes the result of our suffering is a renewed love and dependence on the Father. It is a tremendous blessing to us anytime our faith is strengthened. Unlike Christ, who never struggled in His attitude toward the Father (He and the Father are one), we do struggle with our own attitudes. Yet we are told that the ultimate purpose for our suffering is to be conformed to Christ's likeness. For us to be conformed into Christ's likeness, our immature and imperfect attitudes of trust and faith must be grown and nurtured. Sometimes affliction is the tool God uses to accomplish this result. And He just wouldn't bother if He didn't love us enough to hone our character into what He wants it to be.

Psalm 116:1–7 recounts a time when the psalmist was discouraged and being bombarded with matters of life and death. Yet when he called upon the Lord, God rescued him and blessed him abundantly. The passage says,

> I love the Lord, because he has heard
>   my voice and my pleas for mercy.
> Because he inclined his ear to me,
>   therefore I will call on him as long as I live.
> The snares of death encompassed me;
>   the pangs of Sheol laid hold on me;
>   I suffered distress and anguish.
> Then I called on the name of the Lord:
>   "O Lord, I pray, deliver my soul!"

> Gracious is the LORD, and righteous;
>> our God is merciful.
> The LORD preserves the simple;
>> when I was brought low, he saved me.
> Return, O my soul, to your rest;
>> for the LORD has dealt bountifully with you.

Would he have loved and appreciated the Lord as much if he had never experienced the heavy weight of suffering? Would he have exhorted the Lord's grace and righteousness if those horrific events had never taken place? We can't answer those questions for sure, but I think we can agree that when God rescues us from our circumstances—or our eternal condemnation, for that matter—it demonstrates His love for us. "Though he cause grief, he will have compassion according to the abundance of his steadfast love" (Lam. 3:32).

Blessings in Disguise

Sometimes God places unpleasant circumstances in our lives for our own protection, which demonstrates His love for us. How many times have you heard of something bad happening to someone only to find out that it ended up saving that person's life? The most dramatic example I can think of is the terrible attack on the United States on September 11, 2001. After the smoke cleared, we heard many stories of people who were delayed in some way from going to the Twin Towers that day. Inconveniences? Yes. Illnesses? Yes. Problems? Certainly. But because of those various inconveniences, those people's lives were saved. Whatever their reasons, they were not at work when the attacks took place. God demonstrated His love to them by allowing circumstances that kept them away from danger.

I use this priceless jewel of truth gleaned from the 9/11 attack every day. When I'm late to some event and trying to get there as quickly as I can, I invariably find myself behind the slowest traffic. Although it would be easy for me to experience exasperation and impatience, I try to remember that sometimes God demonstrates His love by sending inconveniences. I recognize that He must be slowing me down for a reason. Remembering this takes the anger out of the situation, and I can rest in His providence. Think about your own experiences. How many times have you had a flat tire, or gotten boxed in between tractor-trailer rigs, or had to pull off and get gasoline when you were already late? Maybe when you finally were able to drive again, you came across several cars pulled over to the side of the road because of a wreck. Perhaps you thought, "If I hadn't had to stop back there, that might have been me!"

Have you ever missed a plane only to find out it had to be diverted way off course because of weather? Have you ever lost a boyfriend and had your heart broken only to find out later that he'd beaten up some other girl? Have you been passed over by a promotion you thought you deserved only to find out later that the position had been outsourced? In each example, the present hardship pales in comparison to the trouble that was avoided. They are all reasons to give thanks in the face of adversity. But even knowing this it's still hard to do, isn't it? Let's face it. We tend to be impatient and ungrateful people. We love to say, "God, if You really loved me, You'd . . ." In these moments, we're no better than impetuous, selfish children.

God never says that He won't take us through difficult places, but He has promised to be with us in those hard times. One of my favorite passages is found in Isaiah 43:1–5,

> "Fear not, for I have redeemed you;
>   I have called you by name, you are mine.
> When you pass through the waters, I will be with you;
>   and through the rivers, they shall not overwhelm you;
> when you walk through fire you shall not be burned,
>   and the flame shall not consume you.

> For I am the LORD your God,
>> the Holy One of Israel, your Savior. . .
>
> Because you are precious in my eyes,
>> and honored, and I love you . . .
>
> Fear not, for I am with you."

He says that we're not going to be kept from the floods or from the fiery trials He brings our way. The blessing is greater than that. The blessing is that *no matter what we must face in this life*, He is right there with us. He even gives us the reason—because He loves us.

Remember King Josiah in the Old Testament? God actually took his life in order to demonstrate His love for him. In 2 Chronicles 34:26–28, we read:

> Thus says the LORD, the God of Israel: Regarding the words that you have heard, because your heart was tender and you humbled yourself before God when you heard his words against this place and its inhabitants, and you have humbled yourself before me and have torn your clothes and wept before me, I also have heard you, declares the LORD. Behold, I will gather you to your fathers, and you shall be gathered to your grave in peace, and your eyes shall not see all the disaster that I will bring upon this place and its inhabitants.

Rather than allow King Josiah to see and experience the devastation God had proclaimed on the nation of Judah, He promised to gather him to his fathers in peace through death. It's the only time I remember God telling someone He was giving death as a gift!

In Conclusion

Perhaps you've heard the saying, "If God seems far off, guess who moved." We don't have to worry about God changing His mind about us day to day. His love for us is constant. We may think that when we are "good," He loves us more than when we are "bad." Not so. Our standing with Him is not that precarious. When we come to understand this truth we'll find it restorative to our souls and soothing to our hearts. As Doug Reed, pastor at Thorncrown Chapel, puts it,

> We may think our standing with God is based on who we are and what we have done. If this is our opinion, we will feel like our favor with the Lord changes from day to day or even from hour to hour. If we measure up, God will bless us; if we don't, He seems far from us . . . Because of Who He is and What He has done, He has become the measure of our favor with God . . . Therefore, *God's kindness towards us never changes*, because the power of the blood of the Lamb never changes. *Jesus is the measure of our standing with God when we do well and even when we fail.*[3] (emphasis added)

This book deals with many purposes of suffering. Overarching all of these purposes for the suffering God brings or allows is His love. His love, compassion, and justice motivate His every dealing with such a sinful group of children as we are. He is slowly conforming us into the likeness of His Son, Jesus Christ, our Savior. He does this because it pleases Him to do so and because He loves us. Why else would He bother? Why not just give us what we deserve and be done with it? Why not cast us all into a fiery furnace for eternity and forget us? The fact that He governs and designs our lives in the first place demonstrates His love for His people. Our Father is worthy of our trust. Let's not doubt Him when times are tough.

Questions for Reflection

1. Why is it important to discipline children? Since we are God's children, why is it important for Him to discipline

us? What does that show us about our standing with Him?

2. Does God have bad days where His mood dictates His actions? What can we always count on where God's judgment is concerned?

3. According to Romans 8:29, what is the purpose of God's working all things to our good (as He promised in Romans 8:28)?

4. God doesn't promise us we'll never suffer. He promises something better! What is that?

5. According to Doug Reed's quote at the end of the chapter, why does our favor with God remain secure, stable, and consistent whether we've failed or succeeded in doing what is pleasing in God's sight?

12

TO DISCIPLINE
HIS WAYWARD CHILDREN

My son, do not regard lightly the discipline of the Lord,
nor be weary when reproved by him. For the Lord disciplines the one he loves, and chastises every son whom
he receives.

—Hebrews 12:5–6

For the moment all discipline seems painful rather than
pleasant, but later it yields the peaceful fruit of righteousness to those who have been trained by it.

—Hebrews 12:11

Godly Discipline

How does this chapter differ from the previous one? The
previous chapter dealt with discipline as a demonstration of
God's love toward us, which is one of the purposes of suffering. This chapter deals with discipline itself as a purpose of
suffering.

As we saw in the previous chapter, because God loves us He will often bring adversity into our lives to discipline us when we are disobedient. Though this can be a prickly subject for some, we must remember that this chastening by God is also intended for our best good as it serves to increase our spiritual maturity and to mold us into whom and what He wants us to be. "Blessed is the man whom you discipline, O LORD" (Ps. 94:12).

Truth or Consequences

Because of God's holiness and justice, He *must* uphold His commands. The concept of holiness has somehow gotten lost in today's society. Holiness can be defined as the state of being spiritually perfect or pure and untainted by evil or sin. But these mere words cannot convey the magnitude of the holiness of God. In the Scriptures, light and darkness are usually used as metaphors signifying good and evil. In 1 John 1:5, we read, "This is the message we have heard from him and proclaim to you, that God is light, and in him is no darkness at all." To put this huge concept in very simple terms, God is completely, totally, and powerfully good and also completely, totally, and powerfully free from all evil, sin, and wickedness. There isn't any darkness in Him at all!

No one can keep God's laws perfectly, but the Bible says we are to live according to those laws. It is not a matter of *if* we break one of them, but a matter of *when*. Seeing that His standard is perfection, it's clear why we needed a savior in the first place. Jesus bore the penalty for our sins on the cross when He exchanged His goodness for our badness—His righteousness for our iniquity. When He gave us eyes of faith and a heart of flesh, we were made right in His eyes in an eternal sense. Our justification is real, eternal, and complete.

But He left us here on this earth, where we are still sinners, even though we are His children. It's surely not shocking to find out that Christians sin. The best of the best are still sinful creatures, graciously forgiven by a loving Father. When we sin, there is an accounting. Disobedience has its consequences, and one of the consequences of our waywardness is God's discipline. Let me remind you that God is just, but He is also merciful. We never get what our disobedience truly deserves. He is patient with us and longsuffering. Yet, there will come a time when, according to His divine plan for our lives, discipline becomes a necessary tool to our repentance.

It's sad that when our lives are rosy our tendency is to deceive ourselves into thinking we are self-sufficient and capable of managing our lives apart from God. That attitude gives us the propensity for sins of the heart, especially the sin of pride. And isn't pride at the root of all sin? After all, we fall away from obedience when we want our way more than God's way. In this way, we sin, become wayward children, and make discipline necessary. Proverbs 13:24 says, "Whoever spares the rod hates his son, but he who loves him is diligent to discipline him." Discipline is an act of love, as we saw in the previous chapter. And if we are wise, we will appreciate the fact that God loves us enough to do it.

> My son, do not despise the LORD's discipline
>   or be weary of his reproof,
> for the LORD reproves him whom he loves,
>   as a father the son in whom he delights. (Prov. 3:11–12)

As imperfect parents, we don't always discipline our children correctly or consistently. We don't confront every infraction, and we shouldn't. Yet, if we are to be strong managers of our households, we are to have high standards of behavior, which requires us to discipline our children when they disobey. But discipline must be executed in a godly, loving way. Even the best parent has to admit that good parenting is one of the most challenging occupations because discipline is difficult. We make mistakes. We overcorrect. We don't correct enough.

117

We're inconsistent. Sometimes we're clueless as to what's going on in our children's heads and hearts. We fail to provide a living example of the biblical principles to which we adhere. Thankfully God is not like us. He is perfect. He is always just and right. He will discipline His wayward children according to our best good and His glory. We do not have the right or the wisdom to second-guess our Heavenly Father. We do not have the right to grumble against His judgments.

One of the purposes of suffering is to grow disobedient children. Through God's righteous discipline, we are brought back into alignment with His will. We must adhere to His commands and His truth or expect consequences. Listed below are consequences suffered by some of God's most faithful servants:

- Moses wasn't allowed to cross into the Promised Land.
- Samson was captured and humiliated by his enemies.
- David's were threefold: the sword never departed from his house, his wives were given to another to enjoy in broad daylight, and the son born to him and Bathsheba died.
- Zechariah became mute until the birth of his son, John.
- Peter experienced intense grief and shame.

In each case, God brought these men to repentance and right relationship with Him. These are dramatic examples, but there are hundreds of smaller examples in our own lives that function in the same way. Each time we suffer the consequences and repent, we are brought into a restored relationship with the Father, which is the goal of discipline.

God Has the Right to Do Whatever He Wants with Us

Remember the example in Romans 9:21 of the potter and the clay? "Has the potter no right over the clay, to make out of the same lump one vessel for honorable use and another for dishonorable use?" God is the potter. The clay has no right to grumble against the one who forms it. The canvas has no right to attack the justice of the painter. The building cannot grumble against the architect who created it.

Job, who started out really well, ended up grumbling against God. And God chose to discipline him by putting him in his place:

> Where were you when I laid the foundation of the earth?
>   Tell me, if you have understanding.
> Who determined its measurements—surely you know!
>   Or who stretched the line upon it?
> On what were its bases sunk,
>   or who laid its cornerstone,
> when the morning stars sang together
>   and all the sons of God shouted for joy? (Job 38:4–7)

He goes on in a similar vein reminding Job that he is creation and not Creator! And that's all it took for Job to repent and throw himself on the mercy of God.

When we have the tendency to grumble at the Lord, we need to be reminded of these truths. In his book, *It's Not Fair!*, Dr. Mack reminds us of these things through meditations on four of the attributes of God—His omniscience (wisdom), His love, His justice, and His omnipotence (sovereignty). Dr. Mack and I collaborated on this book and I heartily recommend it to anyone who has developed a pattern of whining and complaining about their circumstances, or of thinking that God is treating them unfairly.

God is Creator, author of all things, judge of all men, and ruler of the universe. Too many times we question God's justice when it comes to the way He deals with us. Often we like to give Him parameters in which He can work, thinking, "Okay, You can take that away, or refuse me this, but You'd better not touch my husband, or my children, or . . ." We fool ourselves into believing that we can keep a certain person or possession out of God's grasp. We need to ask ourselves, "Who do you think you are?" It's like the mouse who raises his tiny fist to the approaching tractor!

With this in mind, we need to remember that we cannot place God in some kind of box, or limit His options. When He disciplines us, everything is at His disposal. He is well within His right to remove every comfort or possession we have! After all, He doesn't take anything that He didn't give to us in the first place. There is one comfort that He will never take from us though—the comfort and possession of His love and presence.

The Blessing of Discipline

One of the most well known passages about discipline was quoted in the previous chapter from the book of Hebrews:

> *It is for discipline that you have to endure.* God is treating you as sons. For what son is there whom his father does not discipline? If you are left without discipline, in which all have participated, then you are illegitimate children and not sons. Besides this, we have had earthly fathers who disciplined us and we respected them. Shall we not much more be subject to the Father of spirits and live? For they disciplined us for a short time as it seemed best to them, *but he disciplines us for our good, that we may share his holiness.* (Heb. 12:7–10, emphasis added)

It's easy to see the ultimate benefit when we discipline our children. It's sometimes harder to understand and apply the same principle when we view our own discipline at the hands of our loving Father in heaven. Instead of bristling against it, like immature children, we should appreciate it for the same reason that we can rejoice in our sufferings—because of the resulting benefit it brings! It will always result in good and not evil.

○ ○ ○

Questions for Reflection

1. According to Hebrews 12, who does the Lord discipline? Are you His beloved child?
2. What is the one thing God will never take from us?
3. According to Hebrews 12:10, why does He discipline us?
4. Do you remember a time when you may have sulked after receiving His discipline? What should our attitude be toward our Father's discipline?
5. Our natural fathers discipline us because they love us. Why is the Lord's discipline superior to that of our fathers? Does that realization enhance your perception of God's chastening work in your life? Why? Or why not?

13

TO WEAN US FROM THIS WORLD

Do not love the world or the things in the world. If anyone
loves the world, the love of the Father is not in him. For
all that is in the world—the desires of the flesh and the
desires of the eyes and the pride in possessions—is not
from the Father but is from the world. *And the world is
passing away along with its desires*, but whoever does the
will of God abides forever.

—1 John 2:15–17 (emphasis added)

Suffering Clarifies Our Perspectives

Would you like to live your life completely pain-free, problem-free, suffering-free and death-free? Of course you would.
Wouldn't we all? Good news! Those of us who have a relationship of faith with Jesus Christ will get to experience that
existence. It's called heaven!

Ask yourself a question. If you were living in a pain-free,
problem-free, suffering-free world, how anxious would you
be for heaven? If our existence were nothing but roses, then
blissful contentment would be our way of life. *If we were always*

happy, 24 years old, slim, great looking, healthy, wealthy, and wise, how much would we actually look forward to God taking us away from all of that? Not much, you say? That's why I believe that one of the purposes of suffering and death is to make us long for heaven. Heaven is even more a place of *sweet relief* when we are burdened by the cares of this world and the weight of suffering, sickness, death, and grief.

In his tremendous suffering, Job longed for death so he could be out of his misery at last and see the Lord face to face. "For I know that my Redeemer lives, and at the last he will stand upon the earth. And after my skin has been thus destroyed, yet in my flesh I shall see God, whom I shall see for myself, and my eyes shall behold, and not another. My heart faints within me" (Job 19:25–27). Or as the NIV translates it, "How my heart yearns within me." Job yearned for heaven in a far greater way than he had before Satan began his testing.

However, heaven is much more than just a haven for the weary. For the Christian, heaven is a place of greater and greater fascination as we grow in spiritual maturity because we progressively recognize that we will be in full communion with our Lord. His presence is what makes heaven such an incredibly special home for us. A home prepared by the one who secured our very salvation. Those who know God best are the ones who long to be with Him most. The inverse is also true. We are to remember that if we belong to Christ, earth is not our home. We are not to get too comfortable here. Peter wrote in his first epistle, "To God's elect, strangers in the world . . ." (1 Peter 1:1 NIV). The reason we are strangers is because once we're saved, we're merely passing through on a pilgrimage to our true kingdom, heaven. Heaven is our true home.

D. A. Carson reminds us, "Christians ought to be developing a kind of homesickness for heaven."[1] That's where we will dwell with Christ forever. Paul also speaks of our heavenly dwelling in words of longing and eager anticipation saying, "For we know that if the tent that is our earthly home is destroyed, we have a building from God, a house not made with hands, eternal in the heavens. For in this tent we groan, *longing to put on our heavenly dwelling*" (2 Cor. 5:1–2, emphasis added).

I confess that I cannot say I *long* to be clothed with my heavenly dwelling. I do not pray, "Lord, take me now," though, if He does, I'm ready to go. However, I have found that the more I discover about that incredible and amazing place, the more I want to be there. As with so many other things, it's something I'm working toward. I'm not there yet.

Our lives are a journey. During that journey our faith will be tried, our trust will be tested, and our attitudes examined. We are promised safe harbor, that's true, but the journey itself (through the grace of God) will produce the perseverance we need to reach our journey's end, heaven. "*Blessed is the man who remains steadfast under trial*, for when he has stood the test he will receive the *crown of life*, which God has promised to those who love him" (James 1:12, emphasis added).

Suffering takes many forms. For some, the ultimate suffering is physical. They might handle other types of suffering just fine. But they cannot seem to cope with physical pain. For others, the ultimate suffering is emotional. They're troopers when it comes to physical pain but fall apart when their heart gets broken. And for others, the ultimate suffering is spiritual. It grieves them to continue to live in this sinful body apart from the God who saved them (I don't know very many of these, by the way). Regardless of which kind of suffering we must undergo, we all have the responsibility to view that suffering in the light of spiritual truth. The more burdened we are with grief, pain, sorrow, and heartache, the better heaven looks to us. Whatever your idea of absolute suffering may be, it is often that very anguish that brings you to the place where you can say, "Take me, Lord. I long to be with You at last!"

Suffering Causes Us to Loosen Our Grip on the People and Earthly Things We Love

Another aspect of weaning us away from this world is that suffering causes us to loosen our hold on the people and possessions in our lives right now. With our physical eyes, we can see the temporal, the material, and the worldly. But with eyes of faith we become able to glimpse the spiritual and the eternal. With spiritual maturity, we begin the process of turning our focus from worldly, temporal things to heavenly, spiritual things. God gives us grace to stop relying on our subjective feelings and instead to believe and trust His objective Word. Paul says it like this in 2 Corinthians 4:16–18:

> So we do not lose heart. Though our outer nature is wasting away, our inner nature is being renewed day by day. *For this slight momentary affliction is preparing for us an eternal weight of glory beyond all comparison, as we look not to the things that are seen, but to the things that are unseen. For the things that are seen are transient, but the things that are unseen are eternal.* (emphasis added)

On this earth, we have a tendency to latch onto things we love—our families, our homes, our material possessions, our health, our beauty, our wealth, and sometimes even the earth itself in terms of our property. Through suffering, we are sometimes forced to let those things go.

What is seen is transient. It makes no difference how hard we hold on to it. Everything we have can be taken from us. As a reminder of this fact, it might be good to read through the book of Job again. He had it all, and almost all of it was taken from him. His response began well and ended well, but his journey through despair took him to some dreary conclusions, for which he had to repent when God caused him to remember who he was and who God Is.

Our loss may not be as dramatic as Job's, but we all experience it nonetheless. The older we get, the more loss we experience.

We see our vitality, youth, good looks, and health diminish with the passing years. We lose our eyesight, our hearing, our hair, our teeth, and maybe even a couple of organs along the way. Sometimes we lose our fortunes or our homes. Eventually, we may lose our independence, not being able to drive, do our own banking, or even use the bathroom ourselves. But what hurts the most is when we lose the people we love—our parents, our spouse, our friends, and perhaps even our children. Loss is a way of life. We mark it with a series of goodbyes.

An Exercise in Sensitivity

Part of my job is to conduct sensitivity training seminars. One exercise I use helps family members identify with a loved one who is receiving hospice care by illustrating the difficult choices that must be made as one nears death. To begin the exercise I pass out twelve slips of paper to each person and ask them to divide the slips into four sets of three. On the first set, I ask them to write down the three possessions they treasure the most. On the second set, the three personal traits they most appreciate about themselves. On the third set, their favorite three activities. And on the last set, the three people they love the most.

As the exercise continues, I tell them, "You've just been diagnosed with a terminal illness. Get rid of two slips of paper." I pass a little wastebasket around and they must choose two slips to throw away. Everyone has a little trouble with this because they love everything on those slips of paper. Yet, at this point, usually they'll find two they're willing to part with. Then I tell them, "You're getting weaker. You're not able to keep doing all the activities you've enjoyed in the past. Get rid of three more pieces of paper." Now it's getting harder to choose what to give up. Yet, there I am with that wastebasket, standing over them until they decide. This vividly demonstrates that as people get sicker they are really not able to continue with life as usual. They are forced to make these kinds of choices in real life, and it's incredibly difficult. They just don't have the energy anymore.

Next, I tell the participants, "It takes tremendous effort to sit up and carry on a conversation with people. You find yourself sleeping more and the pain forces you to take more medication that makes you feel sluggish. Throw away three more slips of paper." At this point, I begin to see tears in their eyes. Even though it's just an exercise, the symbolism of wadding up and throwing away something or someone they treasure begins to take its toll. Yet, they eventually part with three more and throw them in the hated wastebasket. I proceed. "You're sleeping now more than you're awake. It's harder to keep your eyes open and your mind focused on what's going on around you. Your appetite has vanished and eating only makes you feel sicker. You're refusing food. You are nearing death now. Your chief concern is taking the next breath. Throw away three more slips of paper." The class has gotten very quiet by now. The slips that they must part with are of vital importance. I have no mercy. I stand there with that wastebasket and they must throw them away.

Everyone is left with one piece of paper. Most sit quietly staring at what remains. I explain that a person who has received this kind of diagnosis is similarly faced with losing bits and pieces of who they are, of the things they love, of the activities that have brought them joy, and worst of all, the people they love most. It's a painful process, even for the spiritually mature. Everyone tends to lose the energy it takes to communicate as death approaches. We withdraw from this world slowly and steadily until we don't have the power to open our eyes or squeeze someone's hand. All we can do is lie there and try to keep breathing.

This exercise is extremely effective in helping people identify with the experience of a patient. But it also forces participants to recognize what they hold closest to their hearts, which allows them to empathize with patients on a very personal level. Did they choose correctly? Are they happy with their final choice?

Or did it point to a need in their lives that they should rectify as soon as possible? I never make them share what is written on the last piece of paper. But I do ask them to contemplate their choice briefly before they throw the last slip away.

When we lose a loved one suddenly (stroke, accident, murder, heart attack, etc.), we are forced to lose them without saying goodbye. They are there one moment and not the next. Life is in upheaval and the pain is incredible. But when we lose a loved one through a terminal illness, we say goodbye to them in stages. As they lose pieces of themselves, we lose them too. We say goodbye to their smile or their quick wit. We say goodbye to their independence and must help them in ways we never expected. We say goodbye to their strength, their warm embrace, their interest in our lives, and their input into them. We say goodbye to the sound of their voice, to their advice, and to their stories. By the time they actually die, we find we've been saying goodbye to them for weeks or months before we bid them a final farewell. Is this more painful than losing them suddenly? All I know is that both are excruciating.

The benefit of knowing that death is near is that we're able to walk with them along their journey. We can pray with them, encourage them, do silly things to coax a smile, squeeze their hand, tell them we love them, read the Bible to them, or sing their favorite hymns to them. Whatever form it takes, we have the opportunity to love them through their passage from this life into the next. What an incredible blessing and privilege. If they were believers, their lives were a journey toward heaven. Although we are sad to bid them farewell, we should be content to know that they have finally reached their journey's end. Death, though it appears to be a frightful thing, is a great blessing to them. Death has facilitated their entry into eternity with the Father. We may not be able to see them anymore on our own journey, but we ought to consider that we are traveling toward the same place. Why should it break our hearts that they have gotten there before us? I don't intend to minimize the pain you feel at their passing, but to encourage you to see the event in heavenly terms.

What is the point to all of this? Sickness and suffering (for ourselves or those we love) serve to wean us from this world, from our lives, and from all the hundreds of distractions with which we occupy ourselves when healthy. Illness and suffering help us to gradually let go of our lives, or a loved one's life, when we can't or won't do it on our own. People tearfully ask, "Why is this happening to my mom? She's always been so faithful to the Lord. Why is He letting her linger here like this? Why doesn't He just take her now?" I sometimes remind them that He is not punishing her by leaving her here for a little longer. Instead, He could be helping her family. Often this comment produces a confused look, which prompts me to ask, "If your mother was up and around, walking, talking, and laughing, could you pray that God would take her right now? Would you be ready to let her go?" They shake their heads. "But after watching her slowly drift away from you, you reach the point where you *can* pray that prayer. You're finally at a place where you *can* let her go. Isn't that true?" Most of the time, they agree. Occasionally I hear them later helping their other loved ones with the same truth. Usually, by the time it gets to this point, they don't have too much longer to wait.

This was true of me when I lost my darling brother, John. He was one of my best friends, as well as my cherished brother. When he was healthy and happy, I could never have said, "Lord, please take him." Yet after watching his deterioration from healthy and robust to painfully thin and tormented by the effects of cancer, I was able to reach the place where I could whisper that prayer to the Lord. Because of John's suffering, I was finally able to relinquish my hold on him.

And something else happened as a consequence. Instead of causing me to latch tightly onto my remaining friends and family, I found the ability to hold them with an open hand. I hold them and love them and appreciate every day I'm with them, but if the Lord calls them home, I can let them go. I believe losing my brother has prepared me for such future loss. It will still be hard, but I know that if Christ sustained me through John's death, He will sustain me in the future. He's promised to uphold me with His mighty hand. It is my opinion—from observation and experience—that one of the purposes of the suffering of others is for our benefit. It eventually helps us let go. Then we are able to look beyond our own selfish desire to keep our loved ones near us and instead seek what would be best for them.

Saying goodbye is always difficult, but it becomes more doable after we've watched a loved one drift further and further away from us. Their suffering becomes a blessing to us when we are finally able to entrust them over to death. It helps when the family knows that they're going to a better place, one where they will never suffer again. But, sadly, many do not have that eternal hope. Suffering: the gift of God! Who would have thought it?

He Gave Us Everything We Have

It makes no difference how firmly we grasp the things we love on this earth. Our grip can never be so tight as to keep them out of God's reach. However, it does make a difference in another sense. If we cling to the things of this earth, even trying to keep them from God, we turn them into idols, which the Bible repeatedly warns against. This is something God takes very seriously as is made clear in the following verses:

> You shall have no other gods before me. (Ex. 20:3)

> And he said to all, "If anyone would come after me, let him deny himself and take up his cross daily and follow me. For whoever would save his life will lose it, but whoever loses his life for my sake will save it. For what does it profit a man if he gains the whole world and loses or forfeits himself?" (Luke 9:23–25)

For where your treasure is, there will your heart be also. (Luke 12:34)

... because they exchanged the truth about God for a lie and worshiped and served the creature rather than the Creator, who is blessed forever. (Rom. 1:25)

Yet for us there is one God, the Father, from whom are all things and for whom we exist, and one Lord Jesus Christ, through whom are all things and through whom we exist. (1 Cor. 8:6)

Do not love the world or the things in the world. If anyone loves the world, the love of the Father is not in him. For all that is in the world—the desires of the flesh and the desires of the eyes and pride in possessions—is not from the Father but is from the world. (1 John 2:15–16)

Little children, keep yourselves from idols. (1 John 5:21)

It's easy for us to say, "Oh, I don't worship any idols." However, an idol is anything for which we would sin in order to obtain or keep. Wow! Think about that for a moment and then decide if you have any idols in your life.

An Open Hand

We are to love the Lord, who is to be our all in all, more than anything He has given us. Everything we have is from His hand. We have nothing that He did not give us. Therefore, everything and everyone we love should be lifted up to Him with an open hand. It all boils down to trust. If we completely, totally, absolutely, and always trust the Lord to do what is right, what is just, and what is ultimately for our best good and for His glory, we will be able to trust Him with those we love most. We must trust Him with every beat of our hearts, because He is the one who sustains that as well!

This lesson was brought home to me years ago when my son, Scott, went away to boot camp. Driving back from a tearful goodbye, I heard myself praying, "Lord, he's in Your hands now. Please take care of him." I was shocked! It was as if I had thought because he wouldn't be under my protection anymore that he would now be under God's—as if he hadn't been all along! I had to laugh at my foolishness and confess that Scott had always been under God's protection. There was no more need for worry than there had been before he'd left home!

Therefore, rather than desperately clutching those things we hold dear, we must remember to love the Lord with all our hearts and minds and strength. We must relinquish all things to Him and keep Him uppermost in our hearts. Psalm 73:25 says, "Whom have I in heaven but you? And there is nothing on earth that I desire besides you." Can we honestly say that? Everything we have is a result of God's gracious mercy and generosity to us. It was His to give, and it is His to remove. No matter what He deems best to take from us in His sovereign wisdom, He will never remove the comfort of His love and presence. The people and things of this earth that we love were merely lent to us to serve our own journey; therefore we should set our hearts on heaven as our eternal inheritance. As Job correctly stated, "Naked I came from my mother's womb, and naked shall I return. The LORD gave, and the LORD has taken away; blessed be the name of the LORD" (Job 1:21).

I'm reminded of the passage in Hebrews 10:32–34, which says,

> But recall the former days when, after you were enlightened, you endured a hard struggle with sufferings, sometimes being publicly exposed to reproach and affliction, and sometimes being partners with those so treated. For you had compassion on those in prison, and you joyfully accepted the plundering of your property, since you knew that you yourselves had a *better possession* and *an abiding one*. (emphasis added)

These Christians suffered persecution for the sake of Christ. Regardless of the consequences, they showed compassion to those who had been thrown into prison because of Him. Many times they suffered because of this association and even joyfully accepted the plundering of their property! What? Imagine what your attitude would be if you came home one day and noticed the front door of your house had been broken down and was hanging by one hinge. You run into the house and find it ransacked. All your belongings are gone, even your pictures, books, and furnishings. Everything was taken from you simply because you professed Christianity and sympathized with other believers.

What would you do? Would you sit down on your violated doorstep, cradling your head in your hands, and say, "Woe is me! What am I going to do? What am I going to do? Oh, God, why did You let this happen? What did I do to deserve this? It's just not fair!" Or would you "joyfully accept" such persecution, knowing with certainty that you have a better possession and an abiding one—a personal relationship with Jesus, the King of kings and Lord of lords? Imagine the kind of faith that could do that. Then strive to develop that faith through the power of the Holy Spirit.

Strangers and Exiles

Chapter 11 of Hebrews is made up of people who accomplished great things because of their faith. But their lives were not comfortable and free from pain. Instead, their lives were hard and characterized by suffering. In verses 13–16, we read:

> These all died in faith[2], not having received the things promised, but having seen them and greeted them from afar, and having acknowledged that they were strangers and exiles on the earth. For people who speak thus make it clear that they are seeking a homeland. If they had been thinking of that land

from which they had gone out, they would have had opportunity to return. But as it is, they desire a better country, that is, a heavenly one. Therefore God is not ashamed to be called their God, for he has prepared for them a city.

The people mentioned in this famous hall of faith (Chapter 11) remained faithful through trial; they yearned for their heavenly kingdom. And God promised to prepare for them a heavenly rest, which will be our heavenly rest as well. Our suffering and adversity serve a greater purpose than merely procuring for us the blessings that will result from them. They also cause us to look upward, to turn to Christ, to let go of our earthly possessions, and instead to press onward, holding onto our confidence in Christ.

This concept of life's pilgrimage to our true home can be found in several places in the Bible. One such place is Genesis 47:9: "And Jacob said to Pharaoh, 'The days of the years of my sojourning [pilgrimage] are 130 years. Few and evil have been the days of the years of my life, and they have not attained to the days of the years of the life of my fathers in the days of their sojourning.'" Another is Psalm 39:12: "For I am a sojourner with you, a guest, like all my fathers." To put it in familiar terms, think of any vacation you've ever taken. First, there's travel to your destination. You have already made preparations and have everything you need for your journey. On your way there, you may see beautiful sights and splendid scenery. You might stay at a comfortable and restful hotel, but you are not tempted to take up residence there. Instead, you keep your destination in mind and keep moving toward your goal. You count the lovely experiences, sights, and sounds of the journey as transient pleasures. You're just a tourist, after all, and not a resident of these places. Even though you may meet obstacles and difficulties along the way, you keep pushing toward the goal. You are not tempted to give up when fatigued and settle wherever you come to rest. Your focus, even when you're tired or frustrated, is set on the final destination. That's how we should view our lives on this earth. We are to enjoy the sights but our hearts ought to be fixed on our destination—heaven, our true home.

God doesn't leave us in the dark as to how we are to get there. He reminds us that we have a map to guide us along our journey. In 2 Peter 1:3 we are told, "His divine power has granted to us *all things that pertain to life and godliness, through the knowledge of him* who called us to his own glory and excellence" (emphasis added). He has promised never to leave us or forsake us, and He has given us an invaluable tool in handling adversity with a godly attitude—His Word. This verse teaches that upon the pages of Scripture we are given everything we need. The Bible may not tell us everything we *want* to know, but it tells us everything we *need* to know. And it is through the knowledge of Christ, a knowledge only gotten by careful study of His Word, that we can learn the things that prove so priceless to us when we must face the loss and broken-heartedness that accompany our earthly lives. God has graciously provided for us in so many ways.

In light of this fact, we must keep a godly perspective when it comes to the earthly things we love. Yes, by all means, we should be grateful and should enjoy what God has given us, but we are not to set our hearts and our desires on these things. Instead, we are to live our lives as living sacrifices to God, keeping our eyes unwaveringly fixed on Him. As the hymn writer reminds us, "Turn your eyes upon Jesus. Look full in His wonderful face. And the things of earth will grow strangely dim, in the light of His glory and grace."[3]

○ ○ ○

Questions for Reflection

1. When Christians feel the weight of painful adversity, we lift our eyes to Jesus, who told us to cast our cares and worries on Him. Do you think you would regard Him as

your constant help in times of need if all your needs were automatically met? What benefit does suffering serve in this regard?

2. If you belong to Christ, where is your true home? Do you consider yourself a stranger in this world?

3. Paul wrote in 2 Corinthians 5 that he longs for heaven. In an honest assessment of your own heart, can you say that you also yearn for heaven?

4. What does it mean to hold the things you love with an open hand?

5. The Bible may not tell us everything we _____ to know, but it tells us everything we _____ to know.

14

TO REVEAL SIN IN US

Search me, O God, and know my heart! Try me and know my thoughts! And see if there be any grievous way in me, and lead me in the way everlasting!

—Psalm 139:23–24

Does Suffering Bring Out the Best or the Worst in You?

The above passage, most likely written by King David, is exemplary in its demonstration of godly thinking. David prayed that God would reveal anything offensive in him (that is, sin) so he might repent of it in order to be more pleasing to God.

One of the ways God reveals sin in us is by sending us through trials and suffering. *How we go through adversity says a lot about our inner character.* Do we fret and wring our hands as if there were no God at all? Do we get angry and throw things and lash out at everyone around us? Do we feel sorry for ourselves to the point of despair and hopelessness? Do we blame God and accuse Him of not loving us? These are all indicators of sinful thinking! But these symptoms can help identify what's wrong with us so we can treat it and recover.

I'm wording this as if I were talking about a physical ailment because that's exactly the way it works. If I were to tell a doctor I had a runny nose, watery eyes, a non-productive cough, sneezing, and had been outside earlier rolling in the grass with my kids, she might say I was suffering from allergies. She would tell me what to take to get better, perhaps an antihistamine. But the most effective way of staying healthy would be to stop rolling in the grass, thereby removing the irritant to my system. It works the same with sin. The way we act (or shall I say *re*-act), the way we think, the expressions on our face, the words we say, and our tone of voice can all point to a "diagnosis" of sorts.

The way we respond to adversity reveals much about our spiritual maturity, character, and faithfulness. For example, Proverbs 24:10 says, "If you faint in the day of adversity, your strength is small." The symptom here would be that when adversity hit, you fainted or wimped out. The diagnosis is that your strength is small. In other words, you are a spiritual wimp! I don't think any of us would want to be characterized like that. What's implied is that if you do not want to be counted a spiritual wimp, then don't faint in the day of adversity.

One's specific sin diagnosis might be faithlessness, selfishness, pride, pettiness, arrogance, laziness, jealousy, idolatry, rebellion, or various others. The best way to treat these spiritual maladies is to recognize our sins, repent of them, and remove the irritants that trigger our sinful thinking. We must resist the things that tempt us.

It sounds easy enough, but often it is surprisingly difficult to accomplish. In fact, if we were to try to do it apart from the power of the Holy Spirit, we would fail again and again. Yet since we are commanded to do it, it must be possible. How? Only through the empowering work of the Holy Spirit. This must be a search and destroy mission. We are to search for the iniquity in our hearts and destroy it through genuine repentance. One way God superintends this process is to bring circumstances into our lives that will serve to reveal these sins. Sometimes our trials act like a magnifying glass for our character.

I've heard people say things like, "I've always been such a patient person. But now that my child is a teenager, I find myself losing my patience regularly!" Perhaps a more accurate analysis of this situation is that this person has always been impatient, but it took a catalyst (in this case, his teenager) to reveal this sinful tendency. Most of us who have raised teenagers know that it can be a powder keg of trials and tribulations and can push us to the limit of our abilities. But do we go through this difficult time in our children's lives (and our own) with a godly perspective, or do we lose our cool and resort to yelling or demonstrating our frustrations in other childish and sinful ways? In these cases, God uses our conflicts with our child as a way to reveal our own sin problems. Unless we recognize the problem, we won't seek a solution.

Once we recognize our sin, we can run our repentance based search and destroy program. God guides us to greater spiritual maturity by granting repentance when we confess, which leads us into right thinking and acting. Life is a challenge but we have a step-by-step manual to help us with it. For example, consider 2 Peter 1:3: "His divine power has granted to us all things that pertain to life and godliness, through the knowledge of him who called us to his own glory and excellence." Through careful study, we can learn the principles we are to live by. That includes parenting! Our goal should be to locate the areas in which we sin and to glorify God by turning from them. This is part of our ultimate goal of living a life pleasing to Him. We can strive toward the goal of sinlessness, although we will never completely achieve it this side of heaven. *The blessing is in the striving.*

Remember Proverbs 6:20–23, "My son, keep your father's commandment, and forsake not your mother's teaching. Bind them on your heart always; tie them around your neck. When you walk, they will lead you; when you lie down, they will watch over you; and when you awake, they will talk with you. For the commandment is a lamp and the teaching a light."

An Illustration of the Search and Destroy Method

This is a scenario that happens more times than most of us could imagine. Sam is a strong family man. As a believer he has made sure his family attended church every Sunday. His children are in high school and drive themselves to most of their own functions. They're good kids but Sam realizes that they're more interested in spending time with their friends than with him or his wife, Susan. Susan is a faithful wife and an excellent mother. She keeps a spotless house, prepares fabulous dinners, attends the ladies' Bible study at church, and stays busy with other church activities. She sings in the choir and serves in the youth group as a mentor.

As the years have rolled by, Susan has drifted away from Sam in some ways. She's so busy with all her activities that she's gone several evenings a week. Sam works hard and has always provided for his family. But many times now he comes home from work, eats a quiet meal with Susan, and off she goes to meet her commitments. He watches TV or plays games on the computer to give himself some down time. Because Susan is usually tired by the time she gets home, they are just not as intimate as they once were.

After Sam received his last promotion, he was required to attend meetings with the "big boys" in the company and was occasionally called on to provide information. One of the young, female attorneys who also attended the meetings often smiled at him from across the table. Sometimes she would give him a subtle thumb's up when he was especially impressive. He found this gesture flattering and was pleased that she seemed to pay attention when he spoke. During the breaks, she often sought him out around the coffee bar and lately had begun to fix his coffee for him exactly as she'd seen him do. It is at this point that Sam should have recognized there was more brewing here than just coffee. He should have seen this as a crossroads and nipped this dangerous impropriety in the bud. But he didn't.

Instead, Sam found himself thinking about Olivia more and more. They began to sit together at the meetings and chat about their lives and their interests before and after. Once, Olivia leaned into his shoulder playfully after he'd said one of his famous one-liners and cracked everyone up. He noticed that his reaction to this seemingly innocent gesture was far from innocent. He told himself he'd better watch it but rationalized that there was no real danger. He was a married man, after all, and she was almost young enough to be his daughter. She wouldn't be interested in an old sod like him, and she knew he was married. He'd never made any attempt to conceal it and, in fact, had frequently told Olivia stories about his kids and his wife. At the appreciation banquet for the managers two weeks ago, he'd even introduced Susan to Olivia. Olivia was very warm and respectful to his wife, but commented to her that she was a very lucky woman to have a man like Sam. Susan had smiled and said, "Yes, I know I am. God has been so good to us." Sam had to admit to himself that it embarrassed him when Susan mentioned God like that to Olivia.

Then last week Sam and Olivia went to lunch together. While at lunch, she had two glasses of wine and teased about how she'd better stop or he might try to take advantage of her. He'd laughed, but his mind raced as he wondered if perhaps she was interested in him after all. Olivia made him feel strong, vital, funny, and intelligent. She laughed at his jokes, appreciated all his talents and strengths, and obviously viewed him as a sexy and attractive man. He wondered if Susan ever thought of him like that anymore. She didn't say so. And she certainly didn't seem as genuinely interested in him as Olivia was.

On the way home from work that day, Sam fantasized about how exciting a sexual relationship with Olivia would be. He became aroused just thinking about it and it made him feel good again. He felt like a catch, like a man! When he got home, Susan flashed him a dazzling smile and asked him about his day. She gave him a big hug and immediately he felt guilty for his fantasies about Olivia. He finally realized the wrong direction his mind had taken. While Susan finished setting the table and putting the finishing touches on dinner, he sat in the den and thought about what had happened between him and Olivia.

Suddenly the innocent flirtations between the two of them didn't seem so innocent. He tried to tell himself that if Susan was being the kind of wife she should be, he wouldn't have had these thoughts in the first place. But then came a crushing realization that whether Susan gushed all over him or not, he had made a commitment to her and to God to love only her, forsaking all others. How could he have allowed himself to entertain such sinful thoughts? With his head in his hands, he confessed his sin to God and vowed to turn from it. He knew he had to put a stop to the relationship with Olivia before it went any further. She was a temptation for him, and he had to stop flirting with her (and with disaster) and do the godly thing.

Susan called him to supper, but when he didn't come, she went looking for him and found him in tears in his big leather chair. "What's wrong, honey?" she asked with concern etched on her face. "I love you, Susan," he croaked. "I know that. I love you too. Very much. What's brought this on, Sam?" He stood and held her in his arms for a long time. "We need to talk."

Sam and Susan talked to each other all evening. Sam admitted he felt Susan's interests had shifted away from him and she assured him that she had never meant to leave him out of her life. She apologized and told him she would make sure to do a better job showing her love to him. He told her about Olivia and that he'd repented to God for his behavior. He asked for Susan's forgiveness too, which she freely granted him. By the end of the evening, they felt closer than they'd been in a long time and agreed to start anew in their relationship and give it higher priority.

God blessed Sam and Susan when He brought this realization and renewed commitment. Now they're stronger than ever, and Sam was supremely thankful that God had restrained his sinful behavior and not allowed it to get worse. He followed through with his repentance, which is a turning aside from sin. He strongly explained to Olivia that he had not been acting in a godly manner toward her and asked her to forgive him for participating in such flirtatious behavior. He told her that his wife and family were of great importance to him but of utmost importance was his walk with the Lord. Although Olivia tried to keep the relationship as it was, he made the changes necessary to stay away from her. When she sat next to him at meetings, he'd excuse himself and move to another seat. He made sure they were never at the coffee bar at the same time. He stopped having personal conversations with her and made it clear that their relationship was only professional.

Even though Sam had been unwise and sinful in his behavior and thinking, there were several things he actually did right. He eventually recognized the danger that Olivia posed to him and his relationships with his wife, his children, and his Lord. He repented of both thought and action toward her and completely turned away from his sin. He was honest with his wife and talked out their concerns together. Now their relationship was intimate and fresh and God-centered as it had been so long ago. No, it was better now than it ever had been!

It is unrealistic to think that we will never be tempted. When we begin to think that we are somehow above all that, we enter dangerous territory. "Therefore let anyone who thinks that he stands take heed lest he fall. No temptation has overtaken you that is not common to man. God is faithful, and he will not let you be tempted beyond your ability, but with the temptation *he will also provide the way of escape*, that you may be able to endure it" (1 Cor. 10:12–13). Say with King David in Psalm 101:4, "I will have nothing to do with evil" (NIV). The problem is that sometimes when we meet temptation we don't even look for a way of escape. But rest assured, it's there!

143

Don't Be Afraid to Seek Help in Dealing with Your Sin

God blesses us when He reveals sin in us. Many times we suffer under the burden of sin without even realizing it. Although other people's sins and poor thinking can be truly obvious to us, it is so easy to overlook our own faults, weaknesses, and sins. If we are to clean up our lives (and our thinking) we need our sins to be revealed. Once they're exposed, we can deal with them through the Holy Spirit's empowering work in our hearts, and move on toward greater spiritual maturity.

At times, we may not see ourselves clearly enough, or even when seeing ourselves clearly we may feel unable to deal with our sin without outside help. That's when it's time to "call the doctor" and get some counseling. As I've mentioned before, Bible-based spiritual counseling is so important. Go to someone you view as a man or woman of God, whether they are in a position of leadership in a church or simply a person you respect as being spiritually mature. Talk with them. Be honest with them. Then listen to them and weigh what they tell you. Don't be afraid to ask where their advice can be found in the Scriptures. If it is not supported by the Bible, the advice merely comes from a human mind. This can be a dangerous and infinitely less reliable place to get advice! Keep seeking help until you find someone who can counsel you biblically.

Pray that God will give you the grace, the strength, and the wisdom to fight the sin you're facing and to genuinely repent of it. When you repent, you turn away from sin. True repentance brings real change into your thoughts and actions, as in Sam's example above. However, it is important to realize that though it is your responsibility to repent, it is God who grants such repentance. "And the Lord's servant must not be quarrelsome but kind to everyone, able to teach, patiently enduring evil, correcting his opponents with gentleness. *God may perhaps grant them repentance* leading to a knowledge of the truth" (2 Tim. 2:24–25, emphasis added). Don't be afraid to fall on your knees before the Lord your God. It is there you will find comfort and restoration. God's forgiveness serves as a defibrillator for our faithful walk in grace. Turn to Him and confess your sin. As God promises in Isaiah, "'I dwell in the high and holy place, and also with him who is of a contrite [repentant] and lowly spirit, to revive the spirit of the lowly, and to revive the heart of the contrite. . . . I have seen his ways, but I will heal him; I will lead him and restore comfort to him'" (Isa. 57:15, 18).

Just as physical signs and symptoms point to a physical diagnosis and cure, so also spiritual signs and symptoms brought on by suffering and adversity point to a diagnosis of sin that can be addressed and alleviated through the Word of God. In this respect, the adversity that triggers such a revelation of sin is a tremendous blessing if it moves us closer to our goal of being Christlike.

Questions for Reflection

1. Most of us would rather not think of ourselves in terms of our sins and weaknesses. Have you ever prayed that God would reveal your sins to you so you can repent of them? Will you do that now?

2. What primary sin would you suppose is responsible when a person would rather not know what their sins are? Do you perceive that sin at work in yourself?

3. According to this chapter, what is the best way to stay spiritually healthy and keep sin to a minimum? Is that as simple as it sounds?

4. What is your response to the fact that we are unable to become completely sinless in this life? Does it make you want to quit trying? Does it make you want to strive for the goal anyway? What does the Bible teach about this?

5. If you had to call on a spiritually mature biblical counselor to help you diagnose or treat a spiritual problem, who would you call? Is there someone like that in your life?

15

TO PUNISH THE WICKED

I will punish the world for its evil, and the wicked for
their iniquity.

—Isaiah 13:11

Judgment Belongs to the Lord

This is the last purpose of suffering we will discuss. I have
saved it until the end for a reason. All the other purposes of
suffering we have discussed in this book deal primarily with
the purposes of suffering for believers (though some can also
be a blessing to unbelievers). Jerry Bridges writes in *Trusting
God*, "But this which should distinguish the suffering of believers from unbelievers is the confidence that *our* suffering is
under the control of an all-powerful and all-loving God; *our*
suffering has meaning and purpose in God's eternal plan, and
He brings or allows to come into our lives *only* that which is
for His glory and our good"[1] (emphasis added).

However, God is a God of wrath for those who do not believe
in His Son. John MacArthur writes, "God's wrath is almost
entirely missing from modern presentations of the gospel. It is

not fashionable to speak of God's wrath against sin or to tell people they should fear God."[2] It's just not nice. But sometimes you need to talk about things that are not nice for the sake of those who need to hear it. So, fashionable or not, that's what this section is about.

There are some who choose to only see a God of love and compassion—a sort of grandfatherly God who will rock them to sleep when they're weary. They refuse to see the God of wrath and justice, whose holiness cannot tolerate sin. When we choose to perceive God only as we see fit, then aren't we creating God in our own image instead of accepting what God says about Himself? If we love and honor God, we must see Him with all the attributes of His being, which includes acknowledgment of His wrath. When we water down His righteous anger against sin, we also dilute His holiness.

Where Will You Spend Eternity?

We are all eternal creatures. After suffering physical death here on earth, each of us will enter into an eternal existence on the other side of death. Where we spend that eternity is a different matter. Some will immediately be in the presence of God in a blissful state that will last forever. Others will immediately be separated from God and will spend their eternity in torment and darkness. "For a time is coming when all who are in their graves will hear His voice and come out—those who have done good will rise to live, and those who have done evil will rise to be condemned" (John 5:28–29 NIV). Eternal punishment awaits those who do not place their trust in the Son of God as their Savior. This is a continuing theme in the Bible. Here are only a few of the multitude of verses that teach this:

> The LORD takes vengeance on his adversaries
>   and keeps wrath for his enemies.

The LORD is slow to anger and great in power,
>   and the LORD will by no means clear the guilty. (Nah.
>   1:2–3, emphasis added)

*Inflicting vengeance on those who do not know God and on those
who do not obey the gospel of our Lord Jesus. They will suffer the punishment of eternal destruction, away from the presence of the Lord
and from the glory of his might.* (2 Thess. 1:8–9, emphasis added)

Now I want to remind you, although you once fully knew it, that
Jesus, who saved a people out of the land of Egypt, afterward *destroyed those who did not believe.* . . . Sodom and Gomorrah and the
surrounding cities, which likewise indulged in sexual immorality
and pursued unnatural desire, serve as an example *by undergoing a
punishment of eternal fire.* (Jude vv. 5, 7, emphasis added)

This is the ultimate punishment of hell. But even in this life
God may use the means of suffering to punish disobedience
and wickedness as described in Psalm 107:10–12:

> Some sat in darkness and in the shadow of death,
>   prisoners in affliction and in irons,
> for they had rebelled against the words of God,
>   and spurned the counsel of the Most High.
> So he *bowed their hearts down with hard labor;*
>   they fell down, with none to help. (emphasis added)

There is a happy ending though because in the next two verses
it says,

> Then they cried to the LORD in their trouble,
>   and he delivered them from their distress.
> He brought them out of darkness and the shadow of death,
>   and burst their bonds apart. (Ps. 107:13–14)

In the book of Daniel, we are told that King Nebuchadnezzar ruled over Babylon. Daniel 4:29–32 recounts the story of
his punishment by God:

At the end of twelve months he was walking on the roof of the royal palace of Babylon, and the king answered and said, "Is not this great Babylon, which I have built by my mighty power as a royal residence and for the glory of my majesty?" While the words were still in the king's mouth, there fell a voice from heaven, "O King Nebuchadnezzar, to you it is spoken: The kingdom has departed from you, and you shall be driven from among men, and your dwelling shall be with the beasts of the field. And you shall be made to eat grass like an ox, and seven periods of time [seven years] shall pass over you, until you know that the Most High rules the kingdom of men and gives it to whom he will."

God punished the king because he was taking all the credit for Babylon's greatness and glorifying himself instead of God. The result of this punishment was that after seven years of eating grass with the cattle like a madman, the king lifted his eyes heavenward in repentance and his sanity was restored. Then he praised God and honored and glorified Him, and his kingdom was given back to him. The moral? King Nebuchadnezzar says it himself in Daniel 4:37: "Now I, Nebuchadnezzar, praise and extol and honor the King of heaven, for all his works are right and his ways are just; and *those who walk in pride he is able to humble*" (emphasis added). I'll say! There are many other examples we could examine, but I think you get the point. God punishes the wicked in this life, and without repentance they will ultimately be doomed to a Christ-less eternity. If you do not know the Lord, heed the warnings and promises set forth by His Holy Word.

> Seek the LORD while he may be found;
>   call upon him while he is near;
> let the wicked forsake his way,
>   and the unrighteous man his thought;
> let him return to the LORD, that he may have compassion
>   on him,

and to our God, for he will abundantly pardon.
(Isa. 55:6–7)

Many unbelievers would interpret the word "wicked" in this passage to mean those who are really, really evil, "like Hitler," I often hear. However, that is not the way the Bible uses this term. The wicked are those who do not believe and trust in the Lord Jesus. They are the ones who do not seek to live a life of obedience to Him. You may be a very moral person, in fact, and still be considered among the wicked if you have not come into a saving relationship with Him.

For unbelievers, their suffering serves, in part, as punishment now. Without faith in Christ, their eternal suffering will serve as punishment, in whole, in the life to come. Christians, however, need not dread that judgment. "There is therefore now *no condemnation for those who are in Christ Jesus*" (Rom. 8:1, emphasis added). Praise God.

Questions for Reflection

1. Is there an easy way to tell someone they are bound for hell? Yet it is the most loving thing we could possibly do for someone. Why do you think it is so difficult?
2. What is the difference between punishment and discipline?
3. What or who determines where we'll spend eternity? How so?
4. How did God choose to humble King Nebuchadnezzar? What lesson did he learn from this experience?
5. Who are "the wicked"? Can you be a "good person" by the world's standards and still be numbered with the wicked? Why or why not?

WHAT IS THE BOTTOM LINE?

And we know that *in all things God works for the good of those who love him, who have been called according to his purpose*. For those God foreknew he also predestined *to be conformed to the likeness of his Son*, that he might be the firstborn among many brothers.

—Romans 8:28–29

Trust

As hard as it is to do sometimes, our responsibility as children of the Father is merely to trust Him. Trust Him when you receive a dreaded diagnosis. Trust Him when you lose the job you've held for twenty-seven years. Trust Him when a lightning strike burns your house to the ground. Trust Him when your son goes overseas to fight in a war with which you may not agree.

Why should we trust Him in all these situations? Because of who He is! Because He commands us to. Because He has repeatedly shown us He is worthy of trust. He is all-powerful and almighty yet all-loving and compassionate. He is completely faithful even when we are not. He is completely reliable even though we falter. He loves us in every situation and promises to wield His power to fulfill His purposes in ways that will ultimately benefit us and bring glory to His Name.

We may not like what He brings our way, but through it all we are asked to trust Him. We have to face the fact that He is a God who is so big and so wise that He does things we may not understand. But would we want Him to be any different? Would we really want a God that is more like a glorified genie in a bottle? One who bows to our every demand and desire? If He did that, then who would be God?

Godly Sorrow

Suffering brings us pain, tears, and heartache. He gave us tear ducts for a reason. It's not wrong to grieve, or sinful to be sad. He has never commanded us to be unemotional, unfeeling robots. Yet through our tears, we can still raise our eyes to the Almighty. We can still keep a godly perspective through any trial. Don't think God is oblivious to our tears and our sufferings. As Charles Spurgeon once wrote,

> When a tear is wept by you, think not your Father does not behold, for, "Like as a father pitieth his children, so the Lord pitieth them that fear him." Your sigh is able to move the heart of Jehovah, your whisper can incline His ear to you, your prayer can stay His hands, your faith can move His arm. Oh! think not that God sits on high in an eternal slumber, taking no account of you.[1]

He has given us a useful tool to use whenever we want . . . prayer! Don't underestimate the power of prayer. Our God is a God of means and sometimes our prayers are the very means He will use to bless us if we pray according to His will. He has told us that He hears the prayers of His children, He listens, and He answers.

Sometimes His answer is yes, sometimes it is no, and sometimes it is "not yet." That's why we should be patient in our sufferings and wait on God's perfect timing. When things don't go our way, we're sometimes tempted to question His love for us. When we think of the love of God, we should measure it in terms of a little hill outside the gates of Jerusalem. We should run back to our Bibles and read about the Suffering Servant, the Man of Sorrows. We should remember His flesh, ripped and shredded by a Roman's cruel whip. We should listen for the heavy thud as the cross was dropped into its deep posthole. We should glimpse the blood flowing freely from nail-pierced wounds. We should look into His eyes, burning from the steady flow of mingled blood and sweat from His thorn-pierced brow. We should remember that period of agony as He hung there separated from His Father for the only time in eternity, past and future, clothed with nothing but the filthiness of our sins and iniquity. Would we then dare ask if He really loves us?

When we think like this, shame should rain down on us like black tar, weighing us down until we can do nothing but fall to our knees and confess our sin before a Holy God who has already died for such a sin. When we lift our eyes to the face of our Lord again, we are restored. Oh, Lord, forgive our unbelief!

The bottom line is that regardless of the specific reason for suffering and death in our lives, God is the author and designer of all things that happen to us. God's over-arching purpose for all believers is to conform us to the likeness of His Son, Jesus Christ. He has a unique, tailor-made plan for our individual lives that serves a specific purpose. "Christians will take refuge from their questions about suffering not in bitterness, self-pity, resentment against God, or trite clichés and religious cant, but in endurance, perseverance, and faith in the God who has suffered, who has fought with evil and triumphed, and whose power and goodness ensure that faith resting in him is never finally disappointed."[2]

Suffering and death are powerful tools at His disposal. However, Christians can rest assured that He wields the tools carefully, precisely, lovingly, and always for our best good and for His glory.

In closing, let me quote D. A. Carson from one of his sermons to the Bible Church of Little Rock. It succinctly puts into perspective God's goals for our suffering:

Remember, God is more interested in your *holiness* than in your *happiness*. He's more interested in your *faithfulness* than in your *financial success*. He's more interested in your *purity* than in your *power*. . . . He's more interested in your *eternal life* than in your *external wealth*. He's more interested in your *long-term joy* than in your *short-term fun*. And He's more interested in your *good* than in your *desires*.[3]

The grace of the Lord Jesus Christ and the love of God
and the fellowship of the Holy Spirit be with you all.
2 Corinthians 13:14

Questions for Reflection

1. When we are in the throes of suffering, our primary responsibility as children of God is to _____ Him.
2. Why should we trust Him in any and every situation?
3. What if you don't like the things He brings your way? How will you confront your tendency to resist His will when it differs with your own?
4. According to this chapter, is it wrong to express our sorrow with tears? Do tears indicate a general weakness in faith or character? How can you support your opinion biblically?
5. With what should we measure our Father's love for us?

6. List the parts of this book that you believe will help you the most as you encounter pain and suffering in the future. Write those ideas down on index cards and keep them close at hand for review in the midst of the chaos of tribulation.

NOTES

Chapter One: The Purposes of Suffering

1. D. A. Carson, *How Long, O Lord?* (Grand Rapids: Baker, 1990), 159.

2. John MacArthur (in a sermon at the Bible Church of Little Rock, 1999).

3. Jerry Bridges, *Trusting God Even When Life Hurts* (Colorado Springs: NavPress, 1991), 195.

4. Wayne Grudem, *Systematic Theology* (Grand Rapids: Zondervan, 1994), 811–812.

5. Jerry Bridges, *Trusting God Even When Life Hurts* (Colorado Springs: NavPress, 1991), 52, 101.

Chapter Two: The Origin of Suffering

1. Jerry Bridges, *Trusting God Even When Life Hurts* (Colorado Springs: NavPress, 1991), 209.

Chapter Three: To Complete Our Sanctification

1. Jerry Bridges, *Trusting God Even When Life Hurts* (Colorado Springs: NavPress, 1991), 192.

2. Doug Reed, "Christian Maturity" (Eureka Springs: Thorncrown Chapel, 1997), 12, 19.

3. Jerry Bridges, *Trusting God Even When Life Hurts* (Colorado Springs: NavPress, 1991), 173–74.

Chapter Four: To Drive Our Souls to God

1. Doug Reed, "Christian Maturity" (Eureka Springs: Thorncrown Chapel, 1997), 14.

2. J. C. Ryle, *Ryle's Expository Thoughts on the Gospels* (Grand Rapids: Zondervan, n.d.), 180.

Chapter Five: To Teach Us to Trust God's Promises

1. Richard Baxter, *Dying Thoughts* (Grand Rapids: Baker, 1976), 113.

Chapter Six: To Prepare Us for Coming Glory

1. Charles Spurgeon, "The Sympathy of the Two Worlds," quoted in John MacArthur, *The Glory of Heaven* (Wheaton: Crossway, 1996), 243.

2. D. A. Carson (in a sermon at the Bible Church of Little Rock, 1999).

3. John MacArthur, *The Glory of Heaven* (Wheaton: Crossway, 1996), 100, 104, 106.

Chapter Seven: To Give Us Opportunities to Witness

1. Charles Spurgeon, "Beloved, and Yet Afflicted" (sermon, Dominica: Metropolitan Press, n.d.).

2. John Piper, *A Godward Life* (Sisters: Multnomah, 1997), 19.

Chapter Nine: To Equip Us to Comfort Others

1. Billy Graham, *Facing Death and the Life After* (Nashville: W Publishing Group, 1987), 182.

2. Susan Hunt, *Spiritual Mothering* (Wheaton: Crossway, 1992), 161–62.

Chapter Eleven: To Demonstrate God's Love

1. D. A. Carson (in a sermon at the Bible Church of Little Rock, 1999).

2. Jerry Bridges, *Trusting God Even When Life Hurts* (Colorado Springs: NavPress, 1991), 19.

3. Doug Reed, *Christian Maturity* (Eureka Springs: Thorncrown Chapel, 1997), 18.

Chapter Thirteen: To Wean Us from This World

1. D. A. Carson, *How Long, O Lord?* (Grand Rapids: Baker, 1990), 147.

2. This may refer especially to Abraham, Sarah, and their relatives.

3. Helen Lemmel, "Turn Your Eyes upon Jesus," 1922.

Chapter Fifteen: To Punish the Wicked

1. Jerry Bridges, *Trusting God Even When Life Hurts* (Colorado Springs: NavPress, 1991), 32.

2. John MacArthur, *Ashamed of the Gospel* (Wheaton: Crossway, 1993), 131.

Chapter Sixteen: What Is the Bottom Line?

1. Charles Spurgeon, "The Sympathy of the Two Worlds" quoted in John MacArthur, *The Glory of Heaven* (Wheaton: Crossway, 1996), 239.

2. D. A. Carson, *How Long, O Lord?* (Grand Rapids: Baker, 1990), 246.

3. D. A. Carson (in a sermon at the Bible Church of Little Rock, 1999).